HAVE YOU SUFFERED FROM ANY OF THESE SYMPTOMS IN THE LAST SIX MONTHS?

- Difficulty in getting breath or overbreathing?

- Skipping or racing of the heart?

- Sensation of rubbery or "jelly legs"?

- Bouts of excessive sweating?

- Smothering or choking sensation or lump in throat?

- Tingling or numbness in parts of body?

- Feeling that surroundings are strange, unreal, foggy, or detached?

- Difficulty in falling asleep?

- Avoiding situations because they frighten you?

If you have answered "yes" to one or more of the preceding questions, it is possible that you have a biologically based anxiety disorder that is fundamentally different from the common anxiety that results from specific conditions of stress. This book can help.

Ask your bookseller for these other Bantam Books of interest to readers of THE ANXIETY DISEASE:

FOCUSING by Eugene T. Gendlin, Ph.D.
THE GOOD NEWS ABOUT DEPRESSION
    by Mark S. Gold, M.D.
HEALING VISUALIZATIONS: CREATING HEALTH
    THROUGH IMAGERY by Gerald Epstein, M.D.
HOW TO MEDITATE by Lawrence LeShan
HOW TO RAISE YOUR SELF-ESTEEM
    by Nathaniel Branden, Ph.D.
MINDING THE BODY, MENDING THE MIND
    by Joan Borysenko, Ph.D.

The Anxiety Disease

DAVID V. SHEEHAN, M.D.

BANTAM BOOKS
NEW YORK · TORONTO · LONDON · SYDNEY · AUCKLAND

*This edition contains the complete text
of the original hardcover edition.*
NOT ONE WORD HAS BEEN OMITTED.

THE ANXIETY DISEASE

*A Bantam Book / published by arrangement with
The Scribner Book Companies Inc.*

*PUBLISHING HISTORY
Scribner edition published December 1983
Bantam edition / June 1986*

ISBN 978-0-553-27245-1

Published simultaneously in the United States and Canada

*Bantam Books are published by Bantam Books, a division of Random House,
Inc. Its trademark, consisting of the words "Bantam Books" and the portrayal
of a rooster, is Registered in U.S. Patent and Trademark Office and in other
countries. Marca Registrada. Random House, Inc., New York, New York.*

PRINTED IN THE UNITED STATES OF AMERICA

OPM   30 29 28 27

CONTENTS

Acknowledgments   ix

PART ONE: NORMAL ANXIETY
            AND THE ANXIETY DISEASE   1

   1. The Conflict   3
   2. Two Kinds of Anxiety   8
   3. Who It Strikes and When   11

PART TWO: THE SEVEN STAGES
           OF THE DISEASE   15

   4. Stage 1: Spells   17
   5. Stage 2: Panic   33
   6. Stage 3: Hypochondriasis   39
   7. Stage 4: Limited Phobias   50
   8. Stage 5: Social Phobias   54
   9. Stage 6: Extensive Phobic Avoidance
           (Agoraphobia)   57
  10. Stage 7: Depression   62
  11. Other Complications   66
  12. Frightened Children   71

PART THREE: CAUSES   75

  13. An Interplay of Three Forces   77
  14. Force 1: Biological   81
  15. Force 2: Conditioning   87
  16. Force 3: Stress   97

PART FOUR: TREATMENT   101

  17. The Four Targets of Treatment   103
  18. Diagnosis   108
  19. Target 1: Biological   118

20. Target 2: Phobias   143
21. Target 3: Stresses   149
22. Target 4: Long-term Management   155
23. The Family   162

PART FIVE: THE PHASES OF RECOVERY   167

24. Phase 1: Doubt   169
25. Phase 2: Mastery   174
26. Phase 3: Independence   177
27. Phase 4: Readjustment   179

Further Reading   184
Index   187

ACKNOWLEDGMENTS

Making medicine and psychiatry accessible to the layman while maintaining credible scientific standards requires steering a treacherous course between professional contempt and public misunderstanding. There is a constant struggle between oversimplification for the sake of clarity and a retreat to the caution, endless qualification, and even the obscurity of technical scientific writing. I am indebted to many people for guiding me through the course of writing this book.

I owe a special gratitude to my patients. They shared their special experiences with me and in doing so taught me much of what is useful in this book. I learned to listen to their experiences and take them at face value, especially when they were in conflict with the prevailing perceptions of their condition. They taught me that their disease needed to be taken seriously and not dismissed lightly. They let me see the extent of the tragedy and suffering this disorder can bring by opening their lives to me. Many of them were kind and brave in

ix

volunteering to participate in many of my research projects. Their courageous contributions have helped bring hope to the lives of many other victims of the disease. I feel honored that they provided me with these unique opportunities. I hope that in articulating their special experience and how to cope with it that I can repay a little of the enormous debt I owe them.

Many distinguished medical scientists have made important contributions to the understanding of this disease. Their insights are woven through the pages of this book. Three of these men have had a major influence on my work. I believe that when the history of the investigation of this disease is written, these men will be remembered as giants in the field. Each has made lasting and pivotal contributions to the understanding of this disorder. They are Dr. Donald Klein of New York State Psychiatric Institute, Professor Isaac Marks of London, and Dr. Ferris Pitts of the University of Southern California. Unique contributions to the study of the condition have also been made by professors Max Hamilton, Martin Roth, Malcolm Lader, Michael Liebowitz, William Sargent, and Peter Tyrer of England, and Drs. Russel Noyes, John Clancy, Raymond Crowe, and William Coryell at the University of Iowa. Dr. Joseph Wolpe pioneered the introduction of behavior therapy for anxiety and phobias. Dr. Eugene Redmond of Yale proposed a valuable animal model to study anxiety neurochemically and neurologically. Dr. Charlotte Zitrin's large treatment studies have helped sort out effective from ineffective treatments. Dr. L. Solyom was far ahead of his time in reporting studies of effective treatments before they were fashionable. I am especially indebted to him for drawing my attention to the long-forgotten work and his own contribution to the phenomenon of high arousal regression. The work of all of these scientists has influenced me. I feel honored to have known them, and I value their counsel highly. They have worked tirelessly, often with little reward. Anxious patients everywhere are indebted to their efforts.

I have been very fortunate in my friends and colleagues. I owe a special thanks to two of them. My good friend Dr. Barry Claycomb has spent countless stimulating hours discussing the ideas in this book with me over our many years of collaboration. Indeed many of the ideas in this book are his.

He read through the manuscript and made many valuable improvements. His balanced approach and judgment kept my feet on the ground when my head was in the clouds. Dr. Daniel Carr has taught me much about neurochemistry research. Our discussions on how to unravel the biological mechanisms in the disease have been among the most stimulating experiences of my academic career and offered me a glimpse of the future and of how the mysteries of this disease might be unraveled biologically.

Jim Coleman, director of the worldwide panic project, has been a valuable mentor to me. He has helped find funds for my research, given me valuable advice and guidance, and provided the necessary encouragement, opportunities, and protection for me to do work that would otherwise not have been possible. He is now coordinating the largest single collaboration of international experts ever to investigate this disease. There are very few people who could have engineered such a collaboration with so much energy and skill. Over the years, I have grown personally close to many of his colleagues at the Upjohn Company who have shown me special courtesy and kindness, especially Robert Purpura, Tom Webber, Robert Thompson, Carl Lewis, and Richard Studer. They have valued my efforts even when others were critical. For a young scientist, this is important for his continued best efforts. These men have set an example of how industry can forge a constructive, responsible alliance with academic medicine. This will become increasingly important in the future as industry and medicine work together to unravel the puzzles of medical illnesses and how to treat them more effectively.

I am grateful to Dr. Anthony Reading and Dr. Gerald Klerman for providing me with unique opportunities to pursue my work and for offering me guidance in my career. I owe a debt to Drs. Jim Ballenger and Gary Jacobson, who first introduced me to the problem of agoraphobia. Dr. Timothy Johnson has been most helpful to me. His first-rate medical television programs—"House Call" and later "Healthbeat"—deserve special credit for first bringing accurate medical information on this disorder to national television audiences. Larry and Donna Glick have been very helpful to my research efforts for many years. Through his nationally broadcast radio talk show, Larry has for longer than anyone else I know been a source of comfort and reassurance to agoraphobics everywhere. He has performed a valuable public service even as he entertained his audiences through the night. I am indebted to the Ames family for their many kindnesses to me and for funding the research that led to the clarification of the stages of the disease.

Two people have been invaluable to me in writing this book: my wife, Kathy, and my sister, Una. Their writing skills are much superior to mine, and they have made this work eminently more readable than it otherwise might have been. They tightened up the ramblings in my early drafts and polished up loose prose. They replaced confusion with clarity and kept me on track when I shifted too far off center. Many hours of discussion with them helped me decide what to include and exclude, and how to structure the material for the desired effect. They gave much time to typing drafts and revisions. They have helped me write the book; they deserve a lion's share of the credit.

I always thought that authors only compulsively thanked their editors in the acknowledgments until my collaboration with my superb editor, Michael Pietsch of Scribners, taught me otherwise. A good editor is a blessing to an author. Michael and his copy editor made many improvements while always retaining the essence of what I wished to say. His tactful approach allowed me to sacrifice some idiosyncrasies without bruising my ego and in the interest of producing a better book.

Part One _____
NORMAL ANXIETY AND THE ANXIETY DISEASE

And no Grand Inquisitor has in readiness such terrible tortures as has anxiety, and no spy knows how to attack more artfully the man he suspects, choosing the instant when he is weakest, nor knows how to lay traps where he will be caught and ensnared, as anxiety knows how, and no sharpwitted judge knows how to interrogate, to examine the accused as anxiety does, which never lets him escape, neither by diversion nor by noise, neither at work nor at play, neither by day nor by night.

SOREN KIERKEGAARD, *The Concept of Dread*

For there are . . . sufferings which have no tongue.

PERCY BYSSHE SHELLEY, *The Cenci*

1. *THE CONFLICT*

Maria was heartbroken. She sobbed uncontrollably, holding her head in the pillow to contain her crying. She felt abandoned, misunderstood. People had tried to help, but she knew they just saw her as a brokenhearted, jilted girl.

There was an element of that, of course. But to her the distress was much more fundamental. Something serious came over her body at times that she could not understand or control, yet everyone blamed it on her. She knew it was different from anything she had ever experienced before, but those she spoke to said it was a normal reaction. They thought they understood it. She knew they didn't.

She and Adam had dated for six months. Their relationship had started out warm and friendly, and had developed into a deep love. She felt a strong attraction toward him, a security in his strength. His confidence diminished her self-doubt. He seemed to embody the normality she wished for herself. The closer she was to him, the dimmer her problem became.

3

Everything had fallen apart the day before, when Adam suggested they go to a good restaurant for her birthday. She had felt a cold chill at the thought, and knew that she would spend the next twenty-four hours fearing it. But she also knew that Adam would be disappointed in her if she refused—he'd complained before about how seldom they went out. So she had decided to brave it.

As the hour approached, Maria became more and more anxious. She couldn't think of the restaurant without feeling lightheaded, sweaty, and a little short of breath. The best tables were by a scenic window with that wide-open view out into space and down the steep mountain over the city. What if she lost control and jumped out the window? The thought of falling endlessly down the cliff made her dizzy. Those tables were at the furthest point from the exits. The food was good, the view so spectacular, but the place was always crowded. What if she fainted in front of all those people? They would call an ambulance, and then she would be the focus of everyone's attention. A hundred times she called it off in her mind and felt a relief at the decision. But the thought of not wanting to disappoint Adam always won out. As a special effort she would do it this time for him. He could never really know how much courage that took.

Adam brought her two dozen yellow roses for her birthday, one for each year. That helped her forget for the moment how frightened she had been all day. But the walk from the entrance of the restaurant to the table seemed unusually far. Several times she wanted to turn and run. Although she knew it wasn't so, the whole crowd seemed to look up when she entered and focus upon her. It was as if they were all distracted by the pounding of her heart. She placed her seat so her back was to the window; it made her terribly dizzy to look out. But she felt even more out of control when she faced the crowded room. There were too many people. Was there enough air? She was breathing too fast. Everything around her was becoming strange, unreal, detached. She felt for a moment as if she were looking into the wrong end of a telescope across a misty room.

Maria moved her chair round to face Adam. She would just ride with the feeling until it passed. That's what the books recommended. "You can learn to live with it," was their message. "Stick it out as long as you can," "Don't run away," "Let it pass over you," "It will fade," "Think positive thoughts," "Breathe properly," "Keep going into situations that frighten you until you've conquered the problem." She had tried them all. She hoped someone found them helpful. She had not. The professors who wrote those books just were not on her wavelength. They seemed too caught up in theory to grasp the essence of the real experience.

The menu finally distracted her. She ordered a double Scotch, straight. The waitress and Adam seemed shocked, but she was prepared to accept their disapproval for the relief the drink would bring. She didn't even like alcohol, but it helped dissipate those strange feelings. That's what mattered. Adam chose a good wine. She ate and drank with relish, and Adam took obvious delight in her enjoyment. It was the best she had felt all day.

And then it happened: her heart started beating faster. At first Maria thought it must be the thrill of the occasion, or maybe something in the sauce. Her heart accelerated so fast she could feel the pounding in her chest. She thought Adam must notice. Then the flushing sensation. Her mouth was full. She couldn't breathe properly. Her throat tightened. She felt she was going to choke. Beads of sweat broke out on her forehead; a rushing sensation rose from her stomach up through her chest, then came a sinking sensation in the bottom of her stomach. Everything became detached. She felt dizzy, lightheaded, and then that panicky feeling—that mental panic.

There was no time for explanation. The whole thing was spinning too far out of control. Maria told Adam she had to get out in a hurry, that she would be outside. She couldn't wait around to see what would happen. As she got up, her hand was visibly shaking. Her legs were rubbery. She felt very unsteady, as if she would fall; even the ground was unsteady under her feet. She staggered to the ladies room. Anyone who saw her must have thought she was drunk. The feeling persisted. She went outside to get air.

Adam wanted her to return, but she could not bring herself to do so. His silence on the drive home was unbearable. Later, back at her apartment, Maria tried to apologize and explain that her anxiety condition was getting worse. It nearly crippled her. She just couldn't cope. It made her feel isolated from people, and was making it hard for her even to go to work.

Adam could not, or would not, understand. He was tired of hearing about her anxiety. Why couldn't she just pull herself together and try to overcome it? After all, she wasn't the only person who ever felt anxious. He had had similar experiences, he said, but he knew he had to deal with them directly. That's all there was to it.

Maria tried to tell him that her anxiety was different; it wasn't the same as normal anxiety. She had had normal anxiety in the past, before this thing started. It felt different. Then there had always been a good reason why she felt anxious. But now the attacks came without warning, for no reason at all, even when she was enjoying herself, like tonight, and she could never tell when they were going to hit. It felt like a disease, she said, even though the doctors could find nothing wrong.

It was no good. Adam insisted that she just wasn't trying. He had been too tolerant for too long. First, he said, he'd put up with her neurotic hypochondriacal fears. Then he'd had to humor her through all her little dependencies. Why, she wouldn't even go out anywhere without him. Now, when he brought her somewhere nice, she had to spoil everything with more foolish anxieties. And to crown it all, she was pretending her anxiety was something special. He had had enough. How could he have a relationship with someone who stifled him like this? And how, he asked in a parting jab, could she ever expect to have kids and take care of them and raise them, if she went on with this nonsense?

Maria was crushed. He couldn't have found a better way to hurt her. She had tried so hard all day and had failed totally. She started to cry. She felt guilty. No one understood her problem, not even Adam. Then she couldn't stop crying; it was as if the gates had opened on months of stored tension.

Quietly, she told Adam to go. She had been enough trouble to him already. He told her to call him if she ever straightened out, but not before. Then he left, angry.

Later, though, when he couldn't sleep, Adam thought more about what Maria had said. Maybe he was wrong. Perhaps she did have some condition he had never heard of. Perhaps something could be done for it. On the other hand, maybe she was a neurotic mess and staying with her would just make him a companion to her misery. He went to sleep that night confused and undecided.

The story of Adam and Maria is based on events that have occurred many times and that will undoubtedly be repeated. It encapsulates the plight of a group of the population who are misunderstood by the world of normal people. Adam and Maria are two people polarized by their views of one of man's central experiences: anxiety. Adam doesn't understand Maria's experience of anxiety, although Maria understands his. Since he does not understand, Adam is intolerant of Maria's ways. He even victimizes her in subtle ways, and regards her as inadequate. He does not accept the rules she lives by, but expects her to live by his. Neither can bridge the gap Adam has in embracing Maria's experience. This is the essence of their conflict.

This book is about Maria's people—their plight, their descent into terror, their peculiar experiences. It is also about the beginning of the liberation of these people. And their journey to freedom.

> *The doctrines which best repay critical*
> *examination are those which for the longest period*
> *remain unquestioned.*

ALFRED NORTH WHITEHEAD

2. TWO KINDS OF ANXIETY

Most people, like Adam, regard all anxiety experiences as similar to their own. Extreme cases are usually thought of simply as amplifications of "normal" anxiety. From this assumption it is easy to conclude that all anxiety should be handled in much the same way. If the anxiety is extreme, perhaps more effort is required to deal with it. But it should finally fade, as anxiety always does. It would also seem logical to conclude that it must be triggered by some obvious psychological stress, and that it is really a harmless problem.

But, as Maria's case suggests, there are essentially two kinds of anxiety. The first is the type normally experienced as a reaction to stress or danger, when a person can clearly identify a threat to his (or her) security or safety: a robber puts a gun to his head or the brakes give out on the car. He feels shaky and tremulous. His mouth dries, his palms and forehead sweat, his heart accelerates, his stomach flutters, he tenses up. He experiences mental fear and anxiety. Most people have had these feelings during times of danger or pressure. Similarly, if someone is repeatedly attacked or frightened in a certain situation, he learns to be fearful every time he faces it. It is an ordinary defensive reaction. Repeated bites from an aggressive dog will soon make anyone wary of dogs and fearful in their presence. This anxiety, which is a normal reaction to stress outside the individual, we shall call *exogenous*, or provoked, anxiety. "Exogenous" comes from the Greek words meaning "to be born or produced from the outside." The term reflects the idea that the individual can always identify a justifiable source for this type of anxiety when it occurs.

There is a second type of anxiety called *endogenous* anxiety. This is what Maria has. Adam doesn't understand it; he has never experienced anything like it. Evidence now accumulating suggests that this second anxiety condition is a disease, whose victims appear to be born with a genetic vulnerability to it. It usually starts with spasms of anxiety that strike suddenly, without warning, and for no apparent reason. Sometimes different parts of the body seem to go out of control. The heart may race, or dizziness, choking, shortness of breath, or tingling may occur, even in the absence of any apparent stress or danger. The suddenness of these symptoms, and the fact that they occur without warning, without any clear stress being present, sets the disease apart from otherwise normal response-to-threat anxiety.

"Endogenous" comes from the Greek words meaning "to be born or produced from within." It means literally that the central problem here springs from some source inside the individual's body, rather than as a response to a situation outside the person. This term was chosen to reflect the idea that during some or all panic attacks the victim feels that the episode is coming from within his body, not as a response to external events. In this anxiety disease, as in all diseases, nature has malfunctioned in some way. Like other diseases, it has a life of its own. And it brings misery and suffering.

Normal people often make the mistake of seeing the patient's symptoms as similar to their own reactions when they are stressed or threatened. It is all too easy for those unfamiliar with this disease to underestimate how serious a problem it is, and to think that rest, relaxation, or a good vacation will solve the problem.

In fact, exogenous and endogenous anxiety are really quite different. This book attempts to explain endogenous anxiety, and to show what can be done to help those who suffer from it to live normally again.

"Thus may we see," quoth he, *"how the world wags."*

SHAKESPEARE, *As You Like It*

3. *WHO IT STRIKES AND WHEN*

WHO DOES IT STRIKE?

The anxiety disease affects almost 5 percent of the population at a given time. Approximately 1 percent have it to a disabling degree. The majority (80 percent) of its victims are women, most of whom are in their childbearing years.

The relatively high frequency of the disease among women compared to men has been attributed to a variety of stresses unique to women in our society. Some observers have gone so far as to suggest that the high frequency of the condition among women is directly related to the stress created by women's second-class status in our culture. These theories, while interesting in themselves, fail to explain the remarkable statistical persistence of a predominantly female distribution of the condition over time and space. In all of the countries where the disorder has been studied over the past century, the percentage of women affected compared to men has remained

PHOBIC DISORDERS

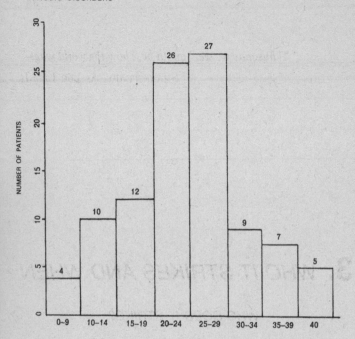

Figure 1. Age of onset of endogenous anxiety

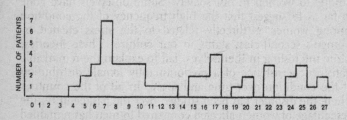

Figure 2. Age of onset of exogenous anxiety

the same. One might expect that wide disparities in women's rights and women's roles would alter this ratio, but such is not the case. And the condition appears to strike equally at women in traditional "homemaker" roles and professional or career women.

WHEN DOES IT START?

If stress alone were the major cause of the anxiety disease, one would expect it to start at any age. After all, stress doesn't appear to pick on any one age group or spare others; each age has its own stresses. So if we examine most conditions in which stress is the primary cause, we find that they can start at any phase in life. But if we look at the age of first onset of this disease, we do not find it spreading itself over all ages. Instead, the majority of cases start in the late teens and early twenties (see Figure 1). It is relatively rare for it to start before the age of fifteen or after the age of thirty-five.

Many diseases have this peculiar attraction to certain age groups. Measles and chickenpox pick on children; high blood pressure usually starts in middle life; strokes and Alzheimer's disease appear somewhat later in life. These peculiar age-of-onset distributions are usually based on some concrete chemical or biological process that permits the disease to favor one age group over others. This is only one of many pieces of evidence that suggest there may be some underlying biological basis to the anxiety disease. Such evidence indicates that although stress plays an aggravating role, as it does in many diseases, biological factors may have a more important role in this disorder than stress alone. (A more detailed discussion of

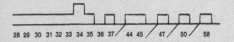

28 29 30 31 32 33 34 35 36 37 44 45 47 50 58

the evidence supporting the metabolic basis of the disease is presented in Chapter 14.)

Normal anxiety displays quite a different distribution. Consider a group of otherwise normal people who have an isolated phobia, for example, a fear of dogs or snakes, or of flying in a plane. These people can usually pinpoint a stress or an upsetting, frightening experience that started the fear. Perhaps they were bitten by a dog, or a close friend died in an air crash. Since these phobias are stress-induced, and stress affects all ages and both sexes more or less equally, we would expect that the onset of these single phobias would be evenly distributed over all ages (Figure 2) and both sexes. This is indeed the case.

The statistics pertaining to endogenous anxiety suggest that nature is at fault in some way. When we find a disease this common that evolution has not extinguished, we have to wonder whether having it confers certain benefits, especially in its mild or attenuated forms. In ways and under circumstances we have not yet discovered, it is possible that having the genetic makeup for this disease may confer some advantage even as it creates misery.

Part Two

THE SEVEN STAGES OF THE DISEASE

I could a tale unfold whose lightest word
Would harrow up thy soul, freeze thy young blood,
Make thy two eyes like stars start from their spheres,
Thy knotted and combined locks to part,
And each particular hair to stand up on end,
Like quills upon the fretful porpentine.

SHAKESPEARE, *Hamlet*

> *It is the part of men to fear and tremble,*
> *When the most mighty gods by tokens send*
> *Such dreadful heralds to astonish us.*

SHAKESPEARE, *Julius Caesar*

4. *STAGE 1: SPELLS*

Maria was twenty-three years old—the peak age for this condition to start—when she had her first spell. She had just finished college and was happily settled into her new job. She was healthy, bright, cheerful, and by all accounts had a good future to look forward to. One evening she was out eating with friends, when suddenly she felt lightheaded, dizzy. It was a feeling that was hard to describe. She felt for a moment as though she were floating off the ground. She excused herself and went to the ladies room, feeling quite unsteady on her legs. She poured cold water on her face, then sat down and rested alone. But she couldn't shake the feeling completely.

When she returned, her friends noted how pale she looked. She dismissed it as just a spell of queasiness, but couldn't quite understand what it was. She had been feeling well; the day had even been uneventful; she wasn't expecting anything unusual. The feeling had come on quite suddenly. She had been discussing their next vacation together with her friends, planning the details of the trip. What could be more pleasant? She was at a loss to find a reason for this feeling. Maybe she was allergic to some additive in the food. It sounded a little like that hypoglycemia she had read about in a magazine. Then again, she was in the premenstrual phase of her menstrual cycle—perhaps it was P.M.S. (premenstrual syndrome). Finally the feeling faded, but she wondered about it a lot afterward.

Maria had almost forgotten about the spell when two weeks later it struck again as she was driving on the highway. Her heart started to accelerate out of control. She could feel it pounding in her chest, thumping in her ears. Her chest and neck throbbed in response. Then suddenly her heart skipped a beat—like hitting a bump in the road when you were driving too fast. Everything jumped up into her mouth for a moment. Having her body run out of control like that was certainly frightening—it could hardly be good for her.

Even though it hit her body in a different place, Maria couldn't help thinking that this spell must be connected to the one she had had in the restaurant. This time it had happened while she was driving somewhere unfamiliar. She hadn't really wanted to go, but she felt a responsibility to see it through. In any event, she realized there was absolutely no reason for it to shake her up to this extent. The spell didn't last as long this time.

She felt fine over the next few weeks. Occasionally, she would have mild, short-lived episodes of a tingling sensation or numbness in her arms or around her face. They didn't bother her much; she just noticed they were occurring more frequently. Sometimes these were associated with the rushing sensation of a hot flash surging up through her body. Obviously she was too young to be getting menopausal, but that's what it felt like. If these little spells continued, she felt she should get them checked out. One part of her mind wanted to consult a doctor; the other self made her hesitate. These spells were so strange. How would she explain them to her doctor? She felt a little embarrassed by them. Maybe he would think her a neurotic young woman troubled by a conflict that was expressing itself in this psychosomatic way. She didn't feel that way about it herself, but she knew from the sound of it that he hadn't much to go on. And if he found nothing, she worried that she might not be taken seriously in the future if she really had something wrong. So she put up with it.

The disease often starts this way, with short spells of symptoms that occur suddenly, spontaneously, without warning and for no apparent reason. This sets it apart from other more common emotional experiences. Frequently these symptoms can occur even without any mental anxiety or panic. Victims feel as if a part of the body has briefly lost control of itself. The delicate workings of the body have temporarily lost their balance.

The spells that occur at this stage can take many forms.

LIGHTHEADEDNESS, FAINTNESS, OR DIZZY SPELLS

"I feel as if I'm going to faint or pass out," is a very common complaint in the early stages of the anxiety disease. This faintness is more like a "white-out" than a "black-out" sensation. It is sometimes associated with a faintly sick feeling and a sensation of fading out from the world. The head may feel literally light. There may be a feeling of weakness in the arms and legs with a sensation of losing some muscular control. In rare cases spinning sensations occur. The feeling causes embarrassment at the thought of becoming the center of attention by fainting in front of others, especially in crowded places.

IMBALANCE AND "JELLY LEGS"

"I'm so unsteady on my feet at times. I'm sure many people must wonder if I've taken to the bottle," explained one lady. "I stagger, having to hold myself up against the wall. When I'm walking, it's as if the ground won't be where I expect it to be. My foot seems to meet the ground at a higher or a lower point than it expects. That throws me off. I feel as if my depth perception is gone. My legs have lost the sense of where they are in space."

Some patients have a feeling that their body is tipped over to one side, and feel a need to compensate for this "leaning tower" feeling. They know objectively they are not tipping over, but in the moment of imbalance why take the risk? It's easy to rationalize it later in the armchair. Others describe the sensation as like walking on the deck of a ship as it is bobbing in high seas. Their footing is never really secure; at any moment they might fall. One man who had this symptom to a marked degree crawled around his house on all fours. As if this was not distressing enough, he felt it necessary to crawl at the angle where the floor met the wall. With his shoulder against the wall and all fours on the floor, he felt more anchored in space and less disoriented. No one knew of his problem. In everyday life he was intelligent, resourceful, successful, and held a position of respect in the community.

A related feeling is that of "jelly legs." In this situation, patients may have extended periods when they feel as if their legs are giving out. They usually need someone to help support them while walking. One patient spent a third of her salary in cab fares to and from work, since her "jelly legs" did not permit her to get there any other way. Once at work, she sat in the same chair literally all day long. She had her lunch brought to her. Her bladder was well trained to survive the day, so she could avoid going to the bathroom until she got home. She had positioned her chair so that it was in the corner of the room at work in the angle of walls and floor. Several times a day she would even need to brace herself into this corner to regain her sense of equilibrium. Because of her problem she was unable to go shopping for clothes. For nine years she wore three dresses and two sweaters in various rotated combinations to work. When she finally came to a doctor about her condition, she had lost the power of her legs completely—she felt they were paralyzed. She came to the doctor in a wheelchair and her faded dress.

Others have described how in trying to walk from one place to another, they have to keep their head down watching the ground closely to ensure a secure footing. "I feel like a drunken sailor in a storm," described one imaginative patient, "but without the benefit of the alcohol."

DIFFICULTY BREATHING

"I have difficulty breathing," "I have difficulty getting to the top of my breath," "I have difficulty getting the right amount of air into my lungs," "I feel like I'm running out of air," or "The air feels thinner," are common descriptions of another type of spell. Patients have described suddenly fearing that they have forgotten how to breathe, that the natural rhythm of their breathing is off, or that if they did not force themselves consciously to breathe, the natural drive to breathe would not exist and they would simply stop breathing. They may feel they are smothering or suffocating. Certain situations are particularly known to aggravate this problem: hot, humid weather, rooms with no windows, closed spaces, and crowding are all well-known and much-feared situations to patients afflicted with these symptoms.

Such spells drive the victim to breathe more deeply and more rapidly. He or she overbreathes—or hyperventilates—taking too much oxygen into the body and blowing off too much carbon dioxide. This leads to a series of changes in the acid-base balance and calcium level in the bloodstream, which in turn leads to several new symptoms—tingling and numbness in parts of the body, lightheadedness and dizziness and finally spasms of the hands and feet and fainting.

Since carbon dioxide provides the signal for the respiratory center in the brain to keep firing, lack of carbon dioxide after overbreathing does the opposite. The respiratory center sees no need to instruct the chest to breathe. After all, it senses that there is too much oxygen already. The patient becomes aware that the normal, regular rhythm of his breathing is gone, and that even the urge to breathe has temporarily left. This frightens him and leads him consciously to start overbreathing further, which only aggravates the problem. A cycle may begin, interrupted finally when the patient faints.

A method commonly used to break this cycle of overbreathing is to have the patient breathe into a paper bag closed tightly around the mouth and nostrils. The oxygen in the bag is quickly used up by the body and the amount of carbon dioxide accumulates. Soon the person is breathing in mostly carbon dioxide, which corrects the acid-base imbalance in the blood set off by overbreathing. It also signals the breathing center in the brain to restore a more normal pattern of automatic breathing again.

Spells of shortness of breath only very rarely lead to this extreme kind of overbreathing. Much more frequent is the feeling of being unable to get the right amount of air into the lungs. At some point in the development of the disease, the majority of patients experience this problem.

PALPITATIONS

Palpitations, which are an awareness of the heart beating, affect the great majority of people with the anxiety disease. It is a frightening and disruptive symptom that involves either skipping of the heartbeat or pounding and racing of the heart. Skipped beats are commonly referred to as "premature contractions." The ventricles are the main chambers of the heart; they normally beat to a regular rhythm. In this disease, the heart muscle may become literally jumpy and contract out of rhythm with the normal beat. This creates the sensation of the heart jumping, or of a double beat followed by a pause that is longer than usual. The heart beats its normal beat, then immediately contracts again too soon. These two beats are felt as twin beats very close together. Since it has worked double time, the heart now takes a longer break before going back to its normal work rhythm again—hence the awareness of a pause before the next beat.

The double beat is often frightening. Some people describe it as a little shock in the chest that causes them to jump and focus their attention inward on their body. Patients often fear that this is the start of a heart attack, or that their heart will become hopelessly irregular and stop. In an anxious individual whose heart is otherwise healthy, such palpitations are common and not considered dangerous.

Frequently, these skips are followed by the heart suddenly deciding to accelerate and race with great speed. Speeds of 140 beats per minute in these circumstances are not uncommon. "Will the heart race so fast it just gives out and stops?" "Will this damage the heart?" and "Can it kill you?" are concerns frequently expressed by people who have to suffer through these episodes. Such fears are often strong enough to lead patients to make extraordinary changes in their lifestyles. One patient moved to live a block from the hospital "for security." She sat in the main hospital lobby, only steps from the emergency room, from before breakfast until late each evening when she left for home and sleep. Her racing and skipping was frequent and severe, and she worried constantly that she would die in the midst of one of these spells. She wanted to be in a position where she could be immediately taken in and resuscitated if her worst nightmare occurred.

The emergency room staff had checked her thoroughly many times. They assured her that she had no serious heart disease; indeed, they explained to her that she merely had an anxiety disorder. Tranquilizers didn't help. On many occasions she had been offered medications that would have effectively treated her condition; however, on checking into each of these, she had read that some of their side effects could temporarily disrupt the heart rhythm and that was enough to cause her to avoid them totally. She learned how to read the elements of EKG machine printouts (the heart machine that reads the rhythm and electrical activity of the heart). When she was feeling well, she spoke of her problem with great insight. She realized only too well that it was anxiety-related, that people didn't die from it, and that she would not come to any harm. She joked about it and made light of it as "pure silliness" in her insightful moments. Yet when it struck again, the insight was quickly abandoned, and surviving the day was her first concern.

After a while she was well known to all the staff. Often, all she needed to do was walk over to the emergency ward, seek out the chief resident, and say, "I'm having one of my attacks again. Just tell me I'm going to be okay and if anything happens to me, you'll know what to do and you won't just leave me to die." At that point the nod and reassuring smile of the chief resident was usually all she needed.

There are several simple ways to slow the heart down when it starts to race. The most well known and perhaps the most effective is massaging the carotid body. The carotid body is a lump that is located on the carotid artery, which carries blood from the heart to the brain; it is found in the neck just below the earlobe at the level of the angle of the jaw. If you place your finger there, you will feel the artery pulsate. Massaging the artery gently at that point causes a reflex slowing of the heart. Never massage both sides together at the same time. The carotid body is full of little receptors that check the rate of the heart and the pressure; if the speed or pressure get out of bounds, they send a signal to the brain to slow the heart by nerve action. Massaging the carotid body tricks it into sending these "slow-down" messages out in greater numbers. The result is that the nervous system works harder to slow the heart rate down. In general, when the heart rate is slower, it is also less likely to produce skips.

Other methods of slowing the heart rate involve taking advantage of a reflex called the vasovagal reflex, also known as the dive reflex. The dive reflex is much more highly developed in primitive animals, especially certain fish. When threatened or in danger, these fish may dive suddenly nose-first to save themselves. The cold water and increased water pressure on their faces stimulates nerve endings in the face and elicits the dive reflex, which causes their heart rate and rate of metabolism to slow down considerably. Their bodies go into low gear as a mechanism of protection and to conserve energy for fight or flight. Man has a vestige of this reflex: stimulating the face, mouth, or throat with cold water, or putting pressure on the closed eyes, will cause some reflex slowing of the heart rate. Many people have found this intuitively when they cool off by putting ice cold water on their face or drinking ice cold water quickly. This technique may be used by victims of heart racing to help slow down their heart rate.

CHEST PAIN OR PRESSURE

In the years after the Civil War in the United States, a physician named Jacob DaCosta, who worked in a military hospital, noted the frequent association between chest pain and anxiety in young soldiers who were upset by their war experiences. He also noted that these young men were otherwise in good physical health and seemed to have no obvious heart disease. This condition, which frequently simulated real heart disease, was later labeled DaCosta's Syndrome, or cardiac neurosis. Often it comes on in the absence of any immediate, obvious pressure or stress, occurring as an isolated symptom when the victim feels no anxiety.

The most common variety is located in the left heart area, often felt deep in the chest under the left nipple. It can penetrate from the left breast area deep into the chest, and sometimes even into the back. A second related variety strikes the right side of the chest above and closer to the center of the chest than the right nipple. Patients use the word "pressure" or "tightness" to describe the feeling. It usually is a deep, dull constant ache. Occasionally a sharp penetrating pain may be superimposed on this. The discomfort frequently forces patients to take deep breaths to expand their chest and try to relieve the pressure. As many as 60 percent of patients with the anxiety disease are troubled by this symptom.

The typical pain of a true heart attack occurs right in the center of the chest and has a crushing, viselike quality. However, the only way to make a good distinction between the two conditions is to have an EKG (a tracing of the heart's electrical activity) during one of these episodes. Knowing that there is no serious abnormality in the heart during such an episode of pain helps put patients' minds at ease, at least about this symptom. In severe cases, patients may feel pain radiating down their left arm, which reinforces their belief that they are indeed having a heart attack.

CHOKING SENSATION

Lisa had lost 40 pounds in weight. She was 122 pounds in college; now she was down to 82 pounds and still losing. It wasn't that she had lost her appetite or gone on a diet. On the contrary, she felt hungry and wanted to eat. But she was too frightened to eat anything but the softest of food. Cheese and ice cream were staples in her diet, and she was even fearful of taking too much of these. "I've got these choking sensations," she explained. "I feel like my throat is going to close over if I eat and that my airway will be blocked. Much of the day there's a lump in my throat. At times this lump suddenly tightens for no reason, even when I'm not eating. I feel something is stuck there. I gasp a little to open it up. When there's food in my mouth, it's much worse." As many as 72 percent of victims of the anxiety disease are troubled by this problem. Lisa's case was of course more extreme than the average. Unfortunately, some people get this sensation so intensely and become so frightened of eating that real choking spells occur. This self-fulfilling fear obviously worsens the problem.

PARESTHESIAS

Paresthesias are tingling sensations or numbness in parts of the body. Two thirds of those with the anxiety disease complain of this symptom. In general it is not particularly distressing in itself, but because the patient associates it with a real disease, the worry that there is something medically wrong causes him more distress than the physical discomfort of the symptom. The tingling sensations are usually located in the arms, hands, feet, or around the face and mouth; sometimes they are marked enough that it feels as if there is a vibrator against the skin. "I feel my lips becoming numbed by the hum sensation," said one patient.

Sensations of numbness are most frequently reported in the arms and sometimes in the face. They may appear to move up and down the arms. "My arms were so numb they almost felt dead. I felt like I lost control over that part of me—I was out of touch with it," described one patient in whom this was the predominant symptom. Another patient who was particularly distressed by this would lose the sensation in half her face, or her right arm or leg would feel dead. On two occasions she had an episode of numbness and weakness in the entire right half of her body. The second time that happened she also lost her voice, and she was sure she was having a stroke. When it cleared up several hours later and the doctor assured her that it was a harmless problem, she found it hard to believe. She checked several medical books, and as a result of her reading, developed a fear that what she had had was the first sign of multiple sclerosis. It seemed so real and dramatic that she thought there had to be a good physical reason for it.

HOT FLASHES

When asked by her doctor to describe her problem, one young woman simply said: "I get these rushes." Another went into more detail: "A sensation of heat starts down low and surges up through my stomach, chest, neck, and face. I feel I'm turning bright red. My face feels hot and flushed." A few patients noted blotching of their skin, especially on the upper chest, following these episodes. At other times they experienced cold chills running through part of them and down their spine. Seventy-two percent of patients with the anxiety disease report these hot/cold sensations.

NAUSEA

Curiously, although as many as 82 percent of patients admit to being bothered by nausea, very few complain of it as their dominant problem. To one patient, it felt like being seasick. Sometimes there may be associated "sinking sensations in the pit of the stomach." "Imagine," said one, "that you have driven over a big hump in the road and you feel your stomach go up and then sink. You know it is happening and that it will be over in a moment. You also know that the reason you feel that way is that you just hit a hump in the road. Now imagine you felt that way, and you didn't have a reason like driving over a hump. And imagine further that you didn't know when or even if it would ever go away. It seemed to go on and on. That's what the experience is like." "After that feeling," said another patient, "throwing up is a relief. It would be a message that it is ending."

These spells may at times make a patient more susceptible to gagging. When he feels the symptom, almost unwittingly he depresses his tongue down into the floor of his mouth and backward into his throat. This brings on increased salivation in the mouth, a sensation of gagging, and an urge to vomit.

A few patients go into periods of prolonged vomiting that they find difficult to stop. Often they require hospitalization to restore the fluids and metabolic balance upset by the vomiting. This problem, too, may be associated with a lack of desire to eat and consequent weight loss, in the attempt not to aggravate the nausea. Others find that eating food actually relieves the feeling, and as a result gain more weight.

DIARRHEA

Ann Marie was the twenty-seven-year-old mother of two, and she wore diapers. It was humiliating, but she had no choice. She felt she couldn't trust her bowels. She would get sudden cramps and a strong urge to move her bowels, and would have to run to the nearest ladies room. If there was none close by, she had an "accident." She had been checked out medically and told that she had no disease of the bowel, but she found she was letting her life get hopelessly restricted by the problem. There were certain things she felt she had to do, like shopping. She knew every bathroom within thirty miles of her house, the choice of her route anywhere being dictated by the proximity of bathrooms.

Ann Marie had to restrict her socializing—she didn't want to monopolize the bathroom everywhere she went. Nor did she want to leave any evidence of the problem after she left. It wasn't the sort of thing your friends cared to hear about, since it was so distasteful. You just had to be practical about it and live with it as best you could. So she did just that. She started wearing diapers and sometimes rubber pants, and restricted herself less. For the most part, none of the diets she had tried had helped significantly. Her poor bowel control was certainly made worse by stress. However, there were other times when she got the attacks with little warning and for no good reason even in the security of her own home. She felt there must be some thread tying this symptom to her lightheadedness and spells of heart racing and shortness of breath. But how, exactly, she couldn't say.

The majority of patients with endogenous anxiety do not get frequent attacks of diarrhea. For those who do get them, they are usually intermittent. Some people are forced to make elaborate ritual preparations before going out. For example, they may feel compelled to restrict themselves to only certain foods or drinks the day before. Bathroom rituals must be observed obsessively. A disruption of the correct order of ritual may throw off all the plans and make it more likely that the expedition will be waylaid by disaster. The condition is frequently called irritable colon syndrome, or spastic colitis.

HEADACHES AND ASSOCIATED PAIN

Eighty-six percent of patients with the anxiety disease are affected by chronic recurrent headaches. It is not unusual to find them using large amounts of aspirin or other pain killers to get through the average day. Their headaches are more stubborn and persistent than the average tension headache. In fact, the pain is not confined solely to the head, but seems more likely to crop up all over, and when it does so, it seems to cause more distress.

It is possible that certain substances in the brain that regulate pain may also be deranged by this disease. When patients have been treated effectively and their condition clears, these pains also clear at the same time. If these people later get a recurrence of their condition, often the very first symptom to recur is the headaches. And if the headaches persist, it is often a warning that bigger spells are yet to come.

OBSESSIONS AND COMPULSIONS

Obsessions are recurrent unwanted impulses, words, or thoughts that persistently intrude on the mind and are hard to get rid of. Usually these are unwanted aggressive, sexual, or poor-impulse-control thoughts. Maria was once sitting in a church and during the quietest part of the service she had a sudden impulse to stand up and scream out a string of obscenities. She was shocked at herself, but she could not shake the thought, and fearing she might lose control, she left the church. Other victims have described being assailed by the sudden thought that they might strangle or harm their child. One patient feared going into a crowded place because she was obsessed with the thought that if she did she would have a panic attack and that to escape the constricted feelings that came with it she would be compelled to tear off her clothes and run naked from the scene.

Since these thoughts are so out of keeping with the rest of the person's usual behavior, the victim is quite horrified by them. Even more troubling for the victim is the fact that the thoughts are hard to shake off and often recur. Some patients come to believe they are losing their sanity and are afraid they will be "locked up" if they report these thoughts to their doctor. When these people learn that many other victims of the anxiety disease have similar thoughts and do not act on them, they are usually surprised and relieved. It is one thing to have such a thought. It is an entirely different matter to act it out.

About 75 percent of the time such thoughts are associated with what are called compulsions, repetitions of the same actions in a rituallike fashion. Repeatedly checking, counting, or washing when it is not necessary are three common examples of compulsive behavior. Frequently these compulsive rituals are attempts to counteract the obsessive thoughts. One woman was plagued by the obsessive thought that she would cause a fire that would destroy her home and kill her family. Each time she was about to leave her home, she felt compelled to engage in a ritual of repeatedly checking ashtrays, her oven, and the other gas outlets, even though she had checked everything fully and thoroughly the first time. She kept doubting that she had checked thoroughly enough.

Obsessions and compulsions are usually not severe symptoms in people with the anxiety disease, and they are less prominent than the other anxiety symptoms. Not all people with obsessions and compulsions are suffering from the anxiety disease. They may have primary obsessive-compulsive disorder, in which there are no anxiety attacks and the obsessions and compulsions predominate over the other symptoms.

DEREALIZATION AND DEPERSONALIZATION

Fifty to 60 percent of patients have symptoms that they find difficult to describe. They will start to explain them and then discover that words can't quite capture the feeling. They may also fear that since it sounds so unusual and bizarre, they will be judged insane. Some have even expressed the fear that they would be committed to an institution.

Derealization means that things around you become strange, unreal, foggy, or detached from you. Said one patient: "I feel I'm in another world. It's like I know I'm there, but I'm really not. I feel removed from the situation I'm in. I feel like I'm in another dimension—like a hollow or vacuum—outside the situation I'm in. It's like watching the whole thing from a distance." And another felt "like I was looking at everything through the wrong end of a telescope—it seemed to get more distant and smaller. Sometimes the opposite would happen and everything would feel closer and larger. One day I was going to cross the street and I got this feeling. I felt that if I stepped off the sidewalk, I would sink into a deep abyss and never make it to the other side of the street, it seemed so far away."

Peter was distressed when he returned to his apartment one evening and had this feeling: "It was like I'd never been there before. Even my roommates looked strange and unfamiliar. One part of me knew I knew who they were and where I was. The other part of me was just alien. It was like I was a fish in a bowl, and they were all around it. I thought I was going nuts, that my mind was splitting and disconnecting from itself. It reminded me of a poem by Emily Dickinson:

> I felt a cleaving in my mind
> As if my brain had split;
> I tried to match it, seam by seam,
> But could not make them fit.
> The thought behind I strove to join
> Unto the thought before,
> But sequence ravelled out of reach
> Like balls upon a floor.

"Sometimes," Peter went on, "I feel like I'm looking at everything around me as if it was through a veil, a fog, or a mist. Sometimes I feel disconnected from the ground under my feet, like I'm walking on air or floating. Last week I was driving my car when I felt that the wheels weren't connected to the road. The car seemed as if it was floating along about two feet off the ground. I felt I didn't have control—I couldn't reconnect with the ground properly. It was scary. It could have caused an accident. The other day was another example. I was walking down the street with my girl friend. I felt my legs were like large springs. When I put my right foot down, I felt the side of my body sink down with my weight, while the other leg elongated with the weight off it. I thought I had to lift my left leg very high to get that foot off the ground. My legs and body felt as if they were bobbing up and down and from side to side on these springs. It was a weird feeling. It must have looked ridiculous. I hope it wasn't too obvious."

Depersonalization is related to derealization. It refers to the sensation of feeling outside or detached from your own body or part of your body. One patient described it as follows: "I was lying awake in bed. The curtains were open and the full moon was out. I was a little frightened, so I held onto my husband's arm for security. He was asleep. Then all of a sudden I couldn't feel him or myself any more. I felt as if I was at the other side of the room looking back at myself in bed. It was as if my spirit had left my body and was looking back at it. Was I dead? I tried to scream for help, but nothing came. Then I remembered reading about 'out-of-body experiences' or 'astral projection.' Maybe I could safely reconnect with myself again. Finally I did. After the experience, I felt it hadn't really happened—only that I dreamed it." She went on to describe a variation of this experience that happened later: "I was walking down the street. All of a sudden it seemed I was out of my body again, but this time I was walking along next to myself."

Such experiences are not uncommon in a lesser degree among the normal population, particularly during adolescence. The hand holding the pen doesn't seem like it's yours; the face in the mirror actually seems like it's someone else's. These derealization and depersonalization experiences are usually but not always a little frightening. The most frequent interpretation patients make of them is that they are losing their sanity and self-control. But such symptoms are not signs of insanity. They are merely common distressing experiences most frequently associated with the anxiety disease.

He fumbles at your spirit
As players at the keys
Before they drop full music on;
He stuns you by degrees.

Prepares your brittle substance
For the ethereal blow,
By fainter hammers, further heard,
Then nearer, then so slow

Your breath has time to straighten
Your brain to bubble cool,—
Deals one imperial thunderbolt
That scalps your naked soul.

EMILY DICKINSON

5. *STAGE 2: PANIC*

Maria continued to have spells intermittently. Then after about three months, her whole condition moved into a new stage: she had a devastating panic attack. It was similar to the spells, but much worse and more frightening.

She was out shopping in a mall when it overcame her. There was nothing special about the evening. Nothing unpleasant had happened to her that day to upset her. She had gone out to window-shop but hoped to find a dress to wear to a party with Adam. She wanted to look her best. Suddenly, unexpectedly, for no immediate apparent reason, her body was overwhelmed by a surge of elemental panic. Everything seemed to race out of control before she could collect her mind to cope with the onslaught. It was like all the spells she had ever had occurring together—and with their power at full force.

Her mind was so overcome, she could feel her vision go off. Everything faded out and became detached, and her

33

heart felt like it wanted to jump out of her chest. She felt very dizzy and lightheaded. Her balance got unsteady. Her legs turned to jelly. The fluorescent lights seemed intensely bright and she seemed acutely sensitive to noise. As she felt beads of sweat break out on her skin, she noticed she was trembling and having difficulty controlling the shaking. She was also acutely short of breath and the tightness in her chest worsened the urge to gasp for air. She felt that if she couldn't get it quickly, she would surely suffocate.

Nothing Maria had ever felt before, even when she was in actual physical danger, had prepared her for this experience. The sheer terror and mental panic were beyond anything she could relate to. It was as if something really terrible was about to happen, or that she was dying but wasn't ready to. She thought that life must extinguish itself in this fashion, that these body changes would quickly signal her death. She had a strong urge to run, but didn't know where or from what. A primitive drive to escape the feeling overwhelmed her. She just dropped the things she was going to buy and ran outside.

In the next five minutes the feeling ran its own course. It seemed to have a life of its own: once started, it would not be deflected, and would stop only when it had spent its energy. Over the next half hour or more Maria still didn't quite feel herself. She was tense and unable to relax, anxious, nervous, and restless. She worried that another attack would strike. She felt very weak, indeed exhausted. Her limbs were heavy, as if they weighed more than they actually did.

Afterwards it was easy to sit back, analyze, and rationalize the experience. Why had she run away when she knew it was inside her body? She couldn't very well run away from a feeling that was inside her, could she? Yet the force of the attack had simply driven her to do just that.

Over the following week, she continued to get occasional spells of symptoms. Each time she feared that they were the advance for the next big panic attack. And a week later it happened again. After that, the panic attacks came approximately three or four times a week. The big attacks were interspersed with little spells of symptoms—about five or six a week.

A few weeks after her first big attack, she was at a play with Adam. They were sitting in the front row of the balcony in the theatre. The play was boring; she noticed how quiet the audience was during one scene. Then she got a panic attack. She felt she was losing control of her mind and was going to stand up and scream in the silent theatre. A moment later she thought her mind would snap: a strong impulse to throw herself over the balcony was coming over her. Since she felt she was losing control of her mind and even going insane, she feared she might act on the impulse. "This feeling that I'm going insane and having bizarre impulses must be a nervous breakdown," she thought. If she wasn't going insane, the whole thing was certainly enough to drive someone insane.

For weeks and months after this she felt as if she was being propelled whimsically toward a cliff and pushed close to the edge. Then, just when she felt she was finished, she would be snatched back—saved for another day's repeat performance.

Maria's experience of unexpected panic attacks is quite a typical one. "You think you know what anxiety and panic are, doctor," patients will say, "but believe me, this is something beyond your experience. You've never had anything like it." Spontaneous panic attacks are clusterings of several spells of different symptoms at once. Their intensity is often greater than during the spells. In addition there is a strong mental terror that accompanies the physical sensation of the body running out of control.

It is puzzling that the majority of patients like Maria have on average between two and four unexpected panic attacks per week. Obviously this can vary, but averaged over long periods of time and over many individuals, it is surprising how constant the figure remains. In female patients, attacks are also more likely to occur premenstrually than at other phases of the menstrual cycle. During this phase they may occur in clusters and with more frequency or intensity.

Many victims are particularly troubled by their sense of loss of self-control. During an attack they feel subject to bizarre impulses, quite out of keeping with their usual character. One patient was very upset and frightened when she was overcome by impulses to harm her son—to push him into a fire or stab him with a knife or scissors. These occurred even at times when the child was not irritating her but was being quite loving. She was so frightened by her thoughts that she locked herself in her room until they passed.

Another young woman was very troubled by tight clothes during her panic attacks. A polo-neck sweater, a tight bra or shirt, elastic around her waist, all magnified her sense of being closed in or constricted and of "having the life squeezed out of her" during an attack. She always wore very loose clothes and as few as possible. During attacks, she had a tremendous urge to tear her clothes off entirely in an attempt to throw off the constricting feeling. She was a very proper woman, and the thought that she might have to do this in some public place upset her and restricted her activities. In spite of her strong scruples about it, though, she said she would do so if she had to to prevent a panic attack from overpowering her.

Many people report that they can temporarily lose their normal critical sense with an attack, and may become more suggestible or sensitive to outside influences at these times. During one research project, volunteer patients were given either an active medication or an inactive placebo for several weeks. At one of the regular weekly meetings with six of the patients, one woman stated that she was fearful of continuing the medication. After taking her second·tablet, the right side of her body became numb and weak; she described it as "briefly paralyzed and insensitive," and feared that this was a warning of a stroke.

The group listened to her description with concern. A week later, three of the five remaining patients had experienced this symptom and worried about a stroke. On checking, it was found that three of the four patients who had experienced spells were on the inactive medication or placebo at the time. They were relieved to learn that other people had the same hypersuggestible experiences, and much of that meeting was spent discussing the issue with considerable insight and detachment.

Those who experience spontaneous panic attacks often seek graphic ways to convey their experience to others—an experience so intensely vivid that it frequently leaves a permanent impression in the mind. One soldier, describing his first panic attack in 1944 almost forty years later, could still recall the time of day and location of the attack, what he was doing at that moment, and who he was with. Five months before, he had participated in one of the first troop waves to land on the Normandy beaches on D-Day. He said the anxiety he felt landing on the beaches was mild compared to the sheer terror of one of his bad panic attacks. Given the choice between the two, he would gladly again volunteer to land in Normandy.

One strong-willed executive had always felt that he had succeeded through his unusual willpower and could deal with anything that came his way. He was annoyed that the panic attacks were getting the upper hand on him. He felt it was necessary to exercise his willpower in mastering fear by flexing it like a muscle. So he chose for the test exercise an experience most normal people would find frightening: parachuting from a plane. If he could master that fear with practice, then surely he could cope with his spontaneous panic attacks.

He took his parachute lessons, made several successful jumps, and even came to enjoy the experience. Nonetheless, his panic attacks continued to overcome the best efforts of his willpower. Any day, he said, if he had to choose between having a bad spontaneous panic attack or jumping from a plane at 10,000 feet, even knowing there was a risk his parachute might not open, he would have no difficulty making the choice. He would jump from the plane any time.

"Imagine," said another patient with a vivid imagination, "that you are walking a tightrope between two skyscrapers like the World Trade Center. You are halfway across when a gusty wind starts to blow. You feel your footing go. You look down. It's a long, long drop to the street below. Try to capture the feelings in your body and mind in that situation. The spontaneous panic attack is even worse, and here's why. On the tightrope you know *why* you're anxious: you can identify things that need to be done to cope. The danger is clear. You are also expecting to feel fear and anxiety. There are no big surprises. On the other hand, with the spontaneous panic attack, it can strike unexpectedly at any time. And worse, you can't identify any good reason for it. You can't pin it on anything. It's a nameless terror. It comes from nowhere and you don't know when it will stop, if ever. Since it can strike any time, anywhere, you are never really safe anywhere. If you invented Hell, you'd have to include this as part of the package."

> *Imagination frames events unknown,*
> *In wild, fantastic shapes of hideous ruin,*
> *And what it fears creates.*
>
> HANNAH MORE, *Balshazzar Part II*

6. STAGE 3: HYPOCHONDRIASIS

Long afterward, every time Maria remembered the hypochondriac stage, she felt an acute twinge of embarrassment— she had made a fool of herself in front of her doctor and the many specialists she had seen. At the same time, she couldn't help feeling a little annoyed with them. After all, they could surely see what she was going through. Perhaps if they had really helped her understand the whole process, she might have been spared many of those embarrassing scenes. Yet she knew that when the panic struck, she was so frightened that in the terror of the moment all reason went out the window, and the urge to seek help and get reassurance was overpowering. She could hardly fault her doctors for that: once again the blame fell squarely on this disease of fear. She was embarrassed in front of her friends and family, too. They had tried to be helpful and to contain it. She knew that at times she had been quite unreasonable. But she honestly felt she couldn't help it.

In the weeks after her unexpected panic attacks started, Maria worried about her health when parts of her body seemed out of control. Surely it meant that something was wrong with her physically? She tried to be sensible, but when she found herself in the middle of the next panic attack, she felt sure she was going to die. At the very least she must have some serious disease. At first, she put off going to the doctor since he would undoubtedly confirm her worst fears, that she had a heart disease she had read about called mitral stenosis.

She had imagined the scene many times in which he told her she had a serious disease. She had even decided how she would dispose of her few possessions. She pictured the doctor telling her, in his most serious manner, that she had mitral stenosis. Giving the disease a name made it less fearsome, more concrete, more predictable. Medical names were good like that, she thought; they were at a higher level than ordinary words. They commanded respect, conveyed power. You knew when the doctor voiced the words that behind them was a mysterious power that was somehow reassuring. At the same time she did not want to hear that she would die young. She hadn't lived yet. She could hear the preacher at her funeral likening her to a flower plucked in full bloom.

Finally, she went to her family doctor. He listened patiently to her story. In the waiting room she had felt dizzy from going over it so many times. He examined her thoroughly and carefully, seeming to take longer over her heart, which raced faster and faster as he listened. She felt flushed but hoped he didn't notice. What was he thinking? What could he hear? Why didn't he say anything? That must mean something bad.

At last he said he would order some tests. "Does that mean it's serious?" she blurted out before she could stop herself. He told her there did not seem to be any obvious evidence of a concrete disease process, but that he would order an EKG and some routine lab tests. He set up another appointment for three days later, when the results would all be back.

Maria knew she would spend the next three days and nights worrying about whether he had set up another appointment in order to break the bad news to her. For those three days she was especially sweet to everyone. She wanted to be remembered fondly by everyone after she died. Each moment

of the day seemed more precious. If she had known of her premature death sooner, she would have lived differently, she thought. How could she best spend the rest of her life? She had resigned herself. She felt strangely at peace during those three days, after the months of terror and panic.

But when she returned to the doctor's office, he told her there was nothing seriously wrong; all her blood chemistry was within a normal range. The only problem was some tachycardia and PVCs on her EKG, which he explained was not considered serious in someone her age without any other overt evidence of heart disease. All it indicated was that she was going through a nervous spell.

Maria was disappointed. She explained that she thought she must have some serious disease, since she had had spells when she was sure she was going to die. But the doctor just advised her to take things easy for a while and try to get away from any stress. He explained that stress could not cause any serious harm, and that she could just set up a time with his secretary whenever she wanted to talk about her worries.

Maria was embarrassed. He had done everything the proper way, though. He checked her out well and seemed genuinely interested in being patient and helpful. But she could tell he was thinking that she was just another neurotic hypochondriac and that her symptoms were just psychosomatic. Her pride was injured.

Two days later, she had another bad panic attack that struck out of nowhere. She couldn't breathe properly and began gasping for air. She was smothering. She knew she was definitely going to die this time. In a flash she lost faith in her doctor. How could he say there was nothing seriously wrong? Here she was dying. This felt like the real thing. Her whole mind and body was passing into another dimension of experience. Everything was fading. She desperately wanted to be saved. She started to bargain with God, even though she wasn't normally very religious. But now she was desperate. She promised that if He saved her this time, she would make it up to Him—being better, doing charity work, anything. Finally the panic passed. She had survived.

Her life did not change much from the way it had been before, but these bargaining sessions were the start of some daily rituals. She blessed herself each morning seven times before going out to work—seven times, no more no less. If she did not do it the right number of times or the right way, it could lead to anxiety and fear. On going to bed at night, she would check that the gas was off exactly five times. After she got into bed, she got up and checked it once more. Each time she would feel it had been checked thoroughly and correctly, but then the nagging doubts would set in. Had she really really done it thoroughly? What if she hadn't and suffocated in her sleep? These doubts would persist and keep her awake. It was easier just to get up and give in to them, to get them out of the way, so she could sleep.

With each panic attack, Maria also had more doubts about her doctor's diagnostic ability. Since they persisted, surely it was time for a second opinion. This time she'd see a specialist. As it was her heart that worried her, she decided to see a heart specialist. She set up an appointment with the chief cardiologist at the university hospital. She didn't tell him about seeing her local family doctor, since she did not want him to be prejudiced.

The specialist carried out all the same tests again and even ordered some more. He performed a two-dimensional echocardiogram, the definitive test for a condition he thought she might have. It was an interesting test—she could see the image of the mitral valve of her heart on the screen. The doctor who did it let her view the whole process and was good enough to explain it all. He thought her heart was in fine health, and pronounced it strong enough for another fifty years. Somehow seeing it all on the screen reassured her. She worried less about her heart after that. She was told she had a cardiac neurosis, or DaCosta's Syndrome.

The following week she had another panic attack. The dizzy spells were bad this time, and she felt a numbness and tingling in her arms that was frightening. The right side of her body remained numb and weak for some time after the attack. She thought it must be multiple sclerosis or, worse still, amyotrophic lateral sclerosis—both progressive and potentially fatal neurological diseases that she had read about. So she decided to consult a neurologist.

This time she underwent a whole different set of examinations: nerve conduction studies, a lumbar puncture, specialized blood tests to detect substances that occur in high quantities in association with multiple sclerosis. Finally, a computerized axial tomography scan of her brain and skull (commonly known as a CAT scan) was ordered. It was, they explained, much more sensitive than an X-ray of the head. It took hundreds of cross-section pictures at different levels of the brain, then integrated them by computer to give a total picture of the brain and a better view of the soft tissues of both brain and skull. She didn't have multiple sclerosis or a brain tumor, they found. Neurologically, she was completely normal.

Maria was getting an education in the process; she hadn't realized medicine had so many extraordinary techniques to delve into the inner workings of the body. She marveled at the ingenuity that went into inventing these probing tools. She also got a shock when she got her medical bill. Her insurance paid 80 percent of it, but even to pay 20 percent of the total ate up several months of her savings. However, she learned that her diagnosis was something called conversion hysteria.

When the lump in the throat persisted, she decided next to consult an ear, nose, and throat specialist. Perhaps it was a cancerous tumor. Again after careful examinations they pronounced her healthy. What she had, they felt, was a condition they called globus hystericus. Just a psychosomatic complaint that lodged in the throat.

But she had forgotten to tell the last specialist about her dizzy spells and imbalance, so she went to another ear, nose, and throat specialist and presented him with the dizzy spells and imbalance spells. Again a careful exam. No obvious disease could be found. This time she was told she had vertigo hysterique. They thought at first it was Ménière's disease, which can produce some similar symptoms. But the final series of tests dismissed that possibility.

A month later, Maria again began to suffocate. She kept gasping for air. She called Adam in a panic, something she was doing with increasing frequency—sometimes as often as several times a day. But this time she begged him to come quickly, saying she wasn't sure she would be alive when he got there. He hesitated at first, but realized this was worse than usual and rushed over. When he arrived, she was unconscious on the floor, her hands and feet twitching in spasms.

He called an ambulance. Maria was rushed to the university hospital, where all the emergency screening procedures proved negative. She quickly regained consciousness, but each time she did so, she would start breathing fast, gasping, and then fainting again. The chief resident pronounced it a classic case of hyperventilation syndrome, and demonstrated the paper bag technique to stop it. In ten minutes Maria was more herself again, and an hour later she left the emergency ward with Adam.

Her general practitioner had been notified of the incident, and the emergency ward staff passed along to him the details of her "doctor-shopping," which Adam had supplied. The doctor set up an appointment to see her, to which Maria went with a mixture of embarrassment and determination to get at the root of the problem once and for all. He told her he did not want her to spend her time and money having an extensive and costly medical work-up when the problem was fairly clear to everyone. There were one or two other rare medical disorders that could present themselves in ways similar to her condition. Pheochromocytoma (a rare hormone-secreting tumor of the adrenal gland) or thyrotoxicosis were possibilities. He would refer her to an endocrinologist who specialized in these matters and he would check her thoroughly for these problems. Because she was troubled by bowel symptoms, he would also send her to a gastroenterologist, a specialist in abdominal complaints, to check into her bouts of diarrhea in more detail and to rule out such rare diseases as carcinoid syndrome, a hormone-secreting tumor in the bowel. But he asked her to agree that if nothing came of this last series of tests, she would see a psychiatrist.

The endocrinologist was very systematic in testing for one possibility after another and eliminating them all. He did find that she had some drop in her blood sugar after four hours on the glucose-tolerance test, a condition called idiopathic hypoglycemia. He said it should not cause her any serious harm, but gave her some dietary suggestions to lessen the problem. Finally, Maria had a condition that showed an abnormal result! She asked for a copy of her test results, so that at last she had something on paper that would show something was wrong.

She went to the gastroenterologist as well. He couldn't find any disease, but called her condition spastic colon syndrome and recommended medications that might help the colon. The active ingredient of these drugs, she learned, was an old medicine called atropine or belladonna. In Italy long ago women used to put the drug in their eyes to dilate their pupils, which was thought to make them more attractive. Hence the name for the drug, "bella donna" (beautiful lady). The drug also dilated the bowel and in this way counteracted the spasm in the colon.

Maria had promised her family doctor that if nothing substantial turned up on her tests, she would see a psychiatrist.

After all these medical consultations, she was dizzy from the number of diagnoses she had been given. Who should she believe? No two people agreed on the same diagnosis. But that only increased her sense of alarm about it. Maybe the next doctor would have another diagnosis that was the correct one, and at last something could be done to help.

She did go to a psychiatrist finally, and in the months of treatment heard him refer to her condition by many names: "anxiety neurosis," "hysteria," "hypochondriasis," "depersonalization disorder," "neurasthenia," "somatization disorder," "conversion disorder." Another psychiatrist she consulted called it "panic disorder." Much later in her illness she saw two psychologists. The first called it a "phobic neurosis"; the second termed it "social phobia" or "agoraphobia" at different times. And there were more.

Meanwhile her condition grew progressively worse. No one found anything serious—that they all agreed on—so she might as well save her money. Given the lengths the doctors had gone to and the many phone calls she had made to them, they had been remarkably kind, patient, and tolerant. But she never did get the feeling that any of them quite understood her condition from the inside or that they had a real answer for it. It seemed to her that the problem was not with the doctors. Perhaps it was that medical science did not yet have the technology to probe this disease fully.

*   *   *

Maria's progression through this stage is a typical one. An obsessive preoccupation with health becomes the focus of concern. One study found that all the patients had previously consulted a physician for their symptoms, and that 70 percent of them had consulted more than ten physicians. Ninety-five percent had consulted a psychiatrist for relief. Yet all were still disabled by their illness. After a series of panic attacks, most patients had a large cluster of symptoms, many so-called hysterical or psychosomatic symptoms, many phobias (avoidance behavior patterns), and preoccupation with their health (hypochondriasis), as well as anxiety and fear.

Scores of different symptoms, affecting many different parts of the body, are found in patients with anxiety disease. This presents the doctor with a difficult problem in making a diagnosis. Because of the wide range of highly varied symptoms typically found, it is one of the great impostors of other illnesses found in medical practice. It invites the physician to carry out costly work-ups and drives the patient to seek many consultations from different specialists. When no obvious physical abnormality can be found for the symptoms, the diagnosis each specialist chooses will often reflect his or her specialty interest.

Maria's case attracted many of the more common labels over a year or so. The solution to the confusion in diagnosis lies in evaluating the total collection of symptoms of the patient and seeing the pattern as a whole rather than as a collection of separate parts. The patient's many varied symptoms can come from different angles and do different things at the same time, and all may appear as separate units. Yet it is a mistake to regard the symptoms as signs of separate illnesses. Integrating them into a single unit makes more sense.

Anxiety disease itself is as old as recorded medical history. It has attracted a wide variety of names or diagnostic labels through the centuries, usually as a result of one or two symptoms being elevated to a disease state in their own right. For much of the last century, most cases of this condition would have been labeled as "hysteria." This word is derived from the Greek word for uterus. Since the condition affected mainly women of childbearing years, it was believed to be caused by a wandering uterus: under certain conditions the uterus would "wander" to a different part of the body and cause a local crowding of organs in that area that triggered the symptoms.

In any natural science there is a problem when something is being described for the first time. It is studied at one point in time and described in detail; this description is then fixed. But the description of a living process has been taken out of context of its natural development over time—how it appeared at one point is presumed to be the way it appears at all other times. So one single process that may go through several stages in its natural progression comes to be seen as several different independent conditions; each stage becomes viewed as a separate unit in itself.

In fact, the whole progression through several stages needs to be viewed as a single process that changes over time. The classification of the Hawaiian parrotfish illustrates this point.

Anyone who has taken a vacation in Hawaii and gone snorkeling or scuba diving there has probably seen parrotfish. These large, gaudy, gentle creatures swarm in over the reef in blue-green, gray, and rust-colored waves, grazing like cattle through the coral. As they were first seen, caught, and described by marine biologists, over 350 different species were thought to have been recorded. Then more recently it was noticed that parrotfish undergo dramatic color changes and even sex changes as they mature. Many species mature through three different color phases, including juvenile, adult, and "terminal phase" colorations. The same color pattern is often shared by male and female.

However, some males and sex-reversed females develop into a terminal phase of "super-males," in which they display a variety of peacock-like colors. This led the biologists studying them to reclassify parrotfish by reducing the number of real species to a small fraction of the original 350 types. And the number of species continues to shrink as it is shown that various fishes previously thought to be different species are actually male and female or young or adult varieties of the same fish.

The anxiety disease was once classified under many types

of anxiety, fear, and hysterical symptoms, when in reality it may be one condition (or a very few) passing through numerous stages as it matures over time. In this book seven stages in the evolution of anxiety disease are described. Previously, it was thought that each of these stages was a separate problem: when patients were seen at different stages, they were given different diagnoses. At each stage labels were readily available, depending on which symptom from their collection they chose to display to the doctor and also on the specialty of the doctor to whom they displayed it. The division of this one condition into seven stages here attempts to reconcile the many previously diverse views. The integrated view that this is all in fact one disease is simple and clear. And it helps to make common sense out of something that both patients and doctors feel is riddled with confusion.

The hypochondriac phase is one of a few phases most patients with the anxiety disease go through. Every patient who goes through it does so in his or her unique way. One, for example, was particularly upset by items in the news media, in newspapers, or on television, about health topics. Rarely a day went by without her coming across some reference to a word that embodied her dreaded fear: cancer. Even though she avoided it, she magnetically found the word where for others it would have passed unnoticed, and it would set her heart racing. Her family was forbidden to use the word in any context. Even discussions on astrology bothered her because she knew one of the astrological signs was Cancer.

When her anxiety was triggered, she would start to examine her breasts. Because she had cystic disease of the breasts (small lumps that came and went), and because her breasts were large, this examination was a time-consuming process. She would focus on what she was sure was a cancerous lump, then insist on her doctor checking her within twenty-four hours. At first he performed biopsies, surgically cutting some lumps out for examination. They were found to be normal. After a half-dozen performances, he decided further biopsies were not in the patient's best interest. But she continued in the same pattern for some years, until her central anxiety disease was treated successfully.

In the final analysis, this hypochondriacal behavior may reflect a desperate drive of frightened people to seek help and to protect themselves from a terror they can neither identify nor understand.

> Why do I yield to that suggestion
> Whose horrid image doth unfix my hair
> And make my seated heart knock at my ribs?

SHAKESPEARE, Macbeth

7. STAGE 4: LIMITED PHOBIAS

Four months after her first panic attack, Maria was in an elevator at work. When she got on, it was crowded; she was squeezed against one wall. It was very stuffy. Suddenly one of those overwhelming panic attacks hit her without warning. For a moment she felt like screaming and thought she was losing control. She just had to get off. What if the electricity went off and the lights went out and the elevator got stuck? She quickly got out at the next floor. It took quite a while for her to settle down. She tried to go on the elevator again a few times, but each time as she approached it, her mind filled with negative thoughts—What if it got stuck? What if it was too crowded? What if it was stuffy and the doors wouldn't open? Then her palms would get sweaty, she could feel a knot vibrating in her stomach. Her heart picked up speed and she worried that that would trigger a major panic attack.

It was easier to take the stairs. But each time Maria avoided the elevator, it became more difficult the next time. The anticipation anxiety started earlier and grew bigger. Avoidance seemed to feed the problem. Soon she not only avoided elevators, she wouldn't even consider the possibility of getting on one, no matter what the circumstances.

If the panic attacks persist, sooner or later most patients develop one or more phobias. Clearly not all phobias in the general population develop this way. What is being described here is the usual progression of events in the course of the anxiety disease. It relates to the development of phobias only in this condition. In general, the more intense and frequent the unexpected panic attacks, the sooner the phobias develop.

The first phobias most patients develop are varied—some fear the humidity and heat, while others fear snow and rain, open spaces, closed spaces. The reason for this variety is simple: it usually depends on where the person happened to be when the first severe unexpected panic attack started. If it occurred in a church, he will fear churches. If he got it in the subway, he will avoid subways. Open spaces, closed spaces, rain, heat, snow, eating steaks, being alone, being in crowds, tall buildings or subways, being on highways, getting lost on winding country roads—anywhere or anything that happens to be around when the panic strikes may become the stimulus for a new fear. The anxiety in effect becomes attached to situations or things by association. If an unexpected spontaneous panic strikes repeatedly in the same situation, then a phobia is even more likely to develop to that situation and to persist. The patient will avoid the situation, since it is only natural to avoid anything associated with increased anxiety.

Similarly, it seems natural to keep doing more of anything that is associated with decreased anxiety. Anxiety has its increases, peaks, and declines. When it peaks, people start to run away from the situation in which they felt the panic. As they are running away, the anxiety has peaked and is dropping, and relief is already setting in. When this sequence repeats itself over and over again, relief is associated with running away and avoidance. Then this pairing also becomes associated as a habit. The nervous system is trained that a good way to feel relief is to run away. Going toward the phobia provokes anxiety; running away is associated with

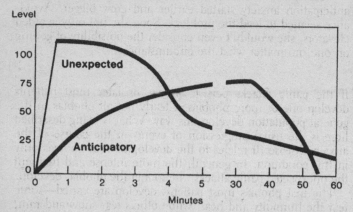

Figure 3. Unexpected and anticipatory anxiety

relief. This will lead to the avoidance becoming more marked over time: avoidance of the phobia in fact feeds the phobia and causes it to grow larger.

This, of course, is not the only way in which phobias are acquired in the anxiety disease. There are several other factors (described in Chapter 15) that may play a role in their onset. But the mechanism described above is a common way many patients describe acquiring their most intense or prominent phobias.

After a phobia develops, patients will often state that they now have two different forms of anxiety. One is the unexpected *spontaneous* anxiety attack. The second we will call an *anticipatory* anxiety attack.

Figure 3 draws a distinction between the two. In the spontaneous anxiety (or panic) attack described earlier, the anxiety surges suddenly, unexpectedly, and for no apparent reason. It seems to overwhelm the body, before the mind can fully figure out how to cope with it. It rushes to peak intensity very quickly. The graph shows the intensity rising to a point above 100 percent. Patients with the anxiety disease insist that this is exactly what it feels like: as if they have passed into another dimension of experience, outside the normal range, that they are fading out, losing control, dying.

Drawing the anxiety's peak at above 100 percent dramatizes the fact that it is beyond the normal person's experience of severe anxiety. Once started, this anxiety has its own life and energy, and seems to be inwardly driven to run its own course. After several minutes it subsides; to the victims it seems like an eternity. Over the next hour or so they gradually recover but feel tense and drained.

An anticipatory anxiety episode, in contrast, is the type of anxiety that comes on in anticipation of something frightening, before the point of real danger. Some patients refer to it as the "what-if" anxiety. "What if I get panicky when I go into that situation?" is the predominant thought. Normal people can understand this kind of anxiety easily as they have usually experienced it. Many normal people have some anticipation anxiety before they go on a stage to make a speech before a large group. As the time gets closer, they feel more restless, the mouth is drier, the heart speeds up a little, the hands are sweaty, there are butterflies in the stomach and perhaps a little tremor in the hand. This increases as the minutes pass and the feared moment approaches.

The graph in Figure 3 shows that the intensity of this anxiety increases gradually. Sometimes it can go higher, but in general it levels off at around 80 percent intensity. There is usually a feeling with this anxiety that it is under mental control to a large extent. At any point you feel that if you were to turn around and run away from the fear you anticipate, the anxiety would quickly subside. It does not have the extreme, bizarre, and terrifying symptom spells that spontaneous anxiety attacks do.

People with the anxiety disease have unexpected attacks at first, and over time gradually acquire more of the anticipatory attacks as they learn new phobias. Normal people cannot understand the unexpected attacks, but they can understand the anticipatory episodes. When these two companions—the unexpected attacks and the anticipatory episodes—join forces, the victim crosses a threshold into a new realm of progressive disability.

Fear has many eyes.

CERVANTES, *Don Quixote*

8. STAGE 5: SOCIAL PHOBIAS

Late one night before their breakup, Maria wrote Adam a letter saying she wanted to end their relationship. It wasn't that she didn't love him enough, but she felt as if she was drowning slowly in the sea of her disease. And she didn't want to bring him down with her.

What had prompted the letter was Maria's inability to join Adam in a series of social situations he wanted her to go to. He had looked forward to them, and she hadn't the heart to tell him in advance that she might not be able to manage. After all, she did have some good days when she was willing to try more things. She had hoped these events would fall on her good days.

The first was a simple evening out to dinner with some of his close friends. But since those panic attacks and choking spells in restaurants—her first had occurred in one—she feared eating out. She was terrified of choking on her food. To protect against this, she could only eat certain things. Then she had to chew the food over and over until her jaws ached—she had to make it soft and eliminate all the "strings" that might stick in her throat and choke her. It was embarrassing. People would notice she was eating slowly and ask if she didn't care for the food. When she chewed excessively, she feared they would notice and ask if the food was too tough. She feared eating and drinking in public. It was now severe enough that she was simply avoiding eating out.

On another occasion Adam was to be presented with an award for his work at an annual banquet. Several people had called to be sure she would come to make the evening a special occasion for him. She knew, though, that since she was a stranger to most of them, she would be a focus of attention. She wanted to avoid being watched and talked about. She never used to feel this way before the condition started; she would have been proud and would have jumped at the opportunity. Now she felt increasingly self-conscious with others. She could sense that her self-confidence had eroded. Would they see her anxiety and sense her self-doubt? Would she lose control and do something embarrassing, like fainting or having to run out?

The week before, she had had to witness some forms at work that were signed by one of the company vice presidents. As she signed her own name, her hand shook visibly. Her signature was hardly recognizable. She held the pen so tightly she felt it dig into the paper a few times. Surely other people must have noticed as they watched. There was simply no reason for her to feel that way, as she normally had felt quite comfortable with the staff. She decided to politely get out of anything like that again.

With the passage of time, as spontaneous panic attacks occur in more situations, more phobias are acquired. The victim learns to associate more and more situations with the attacks. In attempting to escape the panic and the spells, he or she avoids any situations associated with having them. The victim may even avoid situations that place him under mild to moderate stress, since he fears these mildly stressful situations will make his body more vulnerable to a panic attack. When such a surge of panic occurs in the situation, just as he anticipated beforehand, it strengthens his fear of that situation and leads to a new phobia.

Soon he is retreating to security zones. Increasingly he avoids social situations like eating, drinking, or writing in public, being watched or being the focus of attention. He may feel better being alone and in control rather than being with others. He may even feel uncomfortable going places with others and being dependent on them. The retreat to total isolation and disability is only partial at this stage. But the victim can feel the progressive restriction of the disease closing in on him.

The development of phobias is not simply associated with situations in which these patients get spontaneous panic attacks. The spells of Stage 1, if they are frequent, intense, and unpleasant enough, can also bring on phobias precisely in the same way panic attacks do. Attacks of lightheadedness, faintness, imbalance, derealization, and choking are particularly likely to do this. Some patients report that phobias started after the onset of such spells of symptoms, but before the onset of spontaneous panic attacks. When the panic started, this usually sped up the process. In general, however, it is fair to say that there is a progression in which the spells of spontaneous symptoms or of panic occur first and the phobias are a later development. The phobias develop out of one or both of the first two stages. These first two stages are the core. The later stages are complications that develop as a result of that core.

> When sorrows come, they come not single spies,
> But in battalions.
>
> SHAKESPEARE, *Hamlet*

9. STAGE 6: EXTENSIVE PHOBIC AVOIDANCE (AGORAPHOBIA)

After their misunderstanding over her anxiety, Maria didn't hear from Adam for a long while. Her life fell apart. It seemed to her that the dam burst after he left, as if somehow his presence had long put off the disaster she had always feared would occur. The panic attacks came more frequently and intensely. Indeed, collecting new phobias had become a way of life for her. She had so many of them, she could almost say she was phobic of everything. And yet she wasn't really frightened of any of the places or things because of anything inherent in them. What she really felt was that she was frightened of having a bad spontaneous panic attack. That was the center of it. So she had to avoid anything that might bring one on, or had done so in the past.

At one point Maria counted over eighty-five things she was phobic of. The list seemed to grow and grow. She now avoided all crowded places, such as shopping malls or large stores, theatres, church, or sports events. She feared all pub-

57

lic transportation, and couldn't use buses, subways, or trains any more. She feared driving in a car unless it was her own and she was in control: if she had a panic attack, she could just turn back. She found it awkward to apologize to others and to explain why she needed to go back if they were driving. Besides, she didn't like to inconvenience people.

Even so, she could not drive more than five miles from her home. She feared highway driving—there was something about the large open expanse of a highway that upset her. At times it seemed there was just sky everywhere as she drove. She felt momentarily as if she might get sucked out into open space, into infinity up in the sky. She knew it didn't make rational sense. That was the feeling, though, and she wanted to avoid it. And she felt trapped in closed spaces. Although she had always prided herself on her independence, she was now fearful of being alone at home. She even considered advertising for a roommate to cope with this fear. Recently she noticed that she was less anxious in some rooms of her house than others. How much more restricted could she possibly get? What if she got phobic toward her work and had to give up her job? She didn't want to think about it. But she was very determined to fight that off. Already she felt that with all the phobias she had, she was almost at the end of the line.

As the patient continues to suffer more unexpected anxiety attacks and spells, more phobias are acquired, and more situations bring on anticipatory anxiety and are avoided. Anxiety increases; fears spread; confidence diminishes. The more chronic the panic attacks, and the more frequently and intensely they occur, the greater the number of phobias that are acquired. At times the retreat can be so complete that patients will stay in one room of their house.

In one case, after several years of panic attacks, a woman gave up her job and was restricted completely to her house. She feared going out for any reason, even to her mailbox. Not only that, she was restricted finally to one room of her house and even to one piece of furniture in that room. She felt compelled to sit still in a soft chair beside her bed. When she moved off that chair, even toward the door of her bedroom, she could feel the anxiety build up. The bathroom was down the hall from the bedroom. Having to go there was one of the hardest routines of the day—even when she had a strong urge to go, she waited. She suffered the progressive discomfort of a full bladder rather than face the expedition; her natural urge had to be very strong to overcome the fear. The phone was beside her bed. She called her husband frequently during the day begging him to come home. He brought her dinner home every evening and took it up to her bedroom on a tray; they ate there together. He didn't know what else to do.

Patients are usually labeled "agoraphobic" when they have acquired a large number of phobias and are housebound or immobilized to a point where there are few new situations left for them to become fearful of. Agoraphobia is derived from the Greek root word *agora*, meaning a market place or a place of assembly. In Greece, such gathering places were usually crowded open-air marketplaces. For this reason the word "agoraphobia" is sometimes too narrowly interpreted to mean a fear of open spaces. Its real meaning is broader. It refers to fears of crowded places, gathering places, or, in our colder climates, fear of supermarkets and shopping malls.

When psychiatrists and psychologists make this diagnosis, they have found that patients fear any one or all of several things. They fear going far from home (or another point of security) alone, taking public transportation, traveling in a car, going into crowded places, being in large open spaces, or being left alone. When the condition was named, "agoraphobia" was chosen from the cluster of phobias as being one of the most representative or typical of all the many fears the patient has at this point. Curiously, the literal symptom of agoraphobia is not the most common or even central fear shared by patients with the anxiety disease. More common and central is a fear that might be called "phobophobia"—a fear of having another spontaneous panic attack. It is usually this fear that is the most intense and that guides their behavior more than any other fear.

What should be clear is that as far as acquiring phobias is concerned, the agoraphobia stage is the end of the line. Since both Stage 5 (social phobias) and Stage 6 (agoraphobia) tend to be closely associated in time, there is some justification for merging them into one stage of "extensive phobic avoidance." It is often hard for normal people to believe, let alone understand, the extent of some of these fears. Consider the condition of a patient of mine named Jack. He had extreme anxiety "all day long" for many years. This was interspersed with spikes of panic. He was hard pressed to find things he wasn't phobic of; when asked to list his phobias, he wrote simply, "Everything." One day I was going out of state to give a lecture while he was still starting his medication adjustment. He asked if he could have a number to reach me personally in case of emergency. I gave him the number of the convention hotel where the lecture was, in New York City. "But that's a long-distance call from Massachusetts," he said. I assured him that such calls were quite inexpensive. "It's not the expense, doc," he replied, "it's just that I can't make a long-distance call. The thought of my voice carrying that far scares the hell out of me."

Jack could not travel more than three miles in any direction from his home, and the idea of his voice traveling further made him panic. He liked to feel in control. Later he told me that, although he was only in his twenties, he had already bought a lot in the local cemetery up the street for himself. He was sure he was going to die soon, so he wanted to be prepared. But more than that, he wanted to ensure that his body would be buried within his security zone. He panicked at the thought of being buried in some distant cemetery; he worried that somehow he would be in a panic for all eternity if that happened.

Many patients with unexpected anxiety attacks have not yet arrived at this end stage of phobias, although they suffer from the same illness and respond to essentially the same treatment. If their panic attacks persist and remain untreated, they usually progress inevitably through the same course to this stage. This is the reason that some single phobias (like claustrophobia), social phobias, illness phobias, and mixed phobias with panic attacks are considered as earlier stages in the natural history of the disease rather than as separate conditions. In one study, patients with social phobias and agoraphobia had a similar age of first onset. However, when they appeared for treatment, the agoraphobics had had their symptoms for a longer time than the social phobics and were older.

All cases do not follow the same pattern; phobias can be acquired in an order that on the surface defies common-sense logic. One patient was puzzled about what her condition was since it didn't follow any clear-cut pattern she had read about. She was fearful of walking to her mailbox or of driving alone into the local town to go shopping; but accompanied by other people, she could do almost anything. With her husband she flew in planes several times a year to many distant and exotic places without difficulty. However, she did have some unexpected panic attacks and spells. She responded to the same treatment as others with anxiety disease. There was no reason to consider that her condition was any different.

It is often misleading and confusing to focus on the type of phobia a patient has. In making the correct diagnosis and finding the right treatment, it is more helpful to focus on whether these people have spells or unexpected panic attacks in addition to their phobias. Let us consider Michelle's phobias. Her main fear was of storms and tornados. She had once been in a tornado many years before and was terrified by it. Although she lived in a state where tornados and hurricanes were extremely rare, she worried about them daily. In her purse she carried around a small weather radio that was constantly tuned to a twenty-four-hour weather broadcast. She called up the meteorological office regularly for reports and knew the staff there on a first-name basis. She watched the national TV weather reports with great interest once or twice daily, and even videotaped them for replay and closer examinations of the satellite weather pictures.

Michelle had a veritable library of books on meteorological science. Even a tropical storm picking up momentum in the Gulf of Mexico caused her alarm in Massachusetts over 1,000 miles away. If a hurricane started to move through Florida, she was booking a standby ticket to fly a few thousand miles out of the projected path of the storm. She had other phobias. But more important, she had approximately two unexpected panic attacks per week reinforcing and feeding these phobias. For this reason she was considered to have anxiety disease, and she responded very well to drug treatment for this condition.

He straight declin'd, droop'd, took it deeply,
Fasten'd and fix'd the shame on't in himself,
Threw off his spirit, his appetite, his sleep,
And downright languish'd.

SHAKESPEARE, *The Winter's Tale*

10. STAGE 7: DEPRESSION

Shooting and stabbing were too painful. Jumping off a height was too obvious. Hanging was out since she feared choking. Taking an overdose seemed too slow; she might end up a vegetable in the hospital, or she'd have to face everyone with the explanations if she regained consciousness. Maria couldn't think of an easy way to take her own life, but then she didn't try too hard. She was not really set on killing herself; she would just prefer not to wake up, to die passively. She felt sure she had lost Adam, and her phobias had spread to just about everything. She was even getting frightened and panicky at work for no good reason.

Her disability was worsening. She never used to get depressed; now she found herself crying easily. Little things would set her off, and sometimes it was hard to stop the sobbing. Her mood went up and down much more in response to things around her. At times she now felt waves of depressed moods coming over her quickly, often when there was no immediate event to set them off. She would feel hopeless, helpless, and worthless. Then it would go, and she would wonder why it didn't stay.

As Maria was screening these thoughts for what must have been the hundredth time, she was suddenly overcome by a terrifying panic attack. Her heart beat wildly, she began suffocating and gasping for air. She ran to the windows and opened them to let the air in. She felt she was fading out. This was surely it—she was dying. She always knew it would catch up with her someday and kill her. The moment had arrived and she wasn't ready. She prayed frantically, asking God not to let her die yet. She wasn't ready. But the thought flashed through her mind that she could see God looking down and saying, "But only moments ago you wanted to die without a hint of suicide. Now I'm arranging all that for you, and you change your mind. Do you want to live or die? Which do you fear more, living or dying?"

She was recovering from the acute panic now, was being more rational again. That was the irony of the disease. She felt that in her strange world the winds of life and death blew with an energy she had never known before. It was either a wish to die or a desperate wish to live—she was driven from one extreme to the other. But most of all she feared that one day the controls that kept her from the brink of disaster would fail her.

Finally she fell asleep and dreamed she was with Adam, her heart free of fear.

With the progressive disability, the inability to cope with life, work, or family responsibility, or to find an effective treatment, it is not surprising that the victims of this disease become pessimistic and depressed. The majority of patients go through stages of "depression" or feeling downhearted or blue. For this reason many of them have been told that their problem is depression. However, the symptoms of this depression are usually different in type from that seen in the biological depression illness that so often leads to actual suicide and requires antidepressant medication. Indeed, there are a number of antidepressant medications for that kind of biological depression that are not helpful for the anxiety disease or its associated depression. Of course, not all depressions are end stages of the anxiety disease; there are other types of biological depression that occur in the absence of panic attacks.

At this stage, feelings of guilt, hopelessness, helplessness, and worthlessness are common. A negative pessimistic attitude prevails, even toward things that were viewed positively before. These feelings are usually not constant, but come and go like waves that are at times immobilizing. Excessive guilt is particularly common. There is guilt at being unable to cope psychologically with something everyone else thinks one should be able to deal with; guilt at being unable to function as a normal parent or spouse, at not being able to do the routine things all parents do for their children and spouses; guilt at not being able to go shopping, socialize, or engage in leisure activities outside home, eat in restaurants, or travel on vacations. There is guilt at being depressed, helpless, and dependent. Above all, there is guilt at restricting the lives and opportunities of others, especially loved ones, in this web of fear and despair. And the final irony is the guilt at being guilty.

Some patients move progressively through the seven stages over several years; others may be telescoped through several stages quickly in succession. Some manifest one stage more than others or seem to stop at any stage. Some may even remain in one stage for several years before moving on. The critical factor that accelerates progression through these stages is the frequency and intensity of the unexpected panic attacks and spells. Those who start with severe spontaneous panic attacks often quickly acquire many phobias and become depressed. The milder the spells or panic attacks, the more likely the disease will not progress to a later stage. Not all cases of anxiety disease are as severe as Maria's. They frequently occur in milder forms and do not always progress to produce all the complications that Maria suffered.

Stages may move forward and then recede as the patient's condition worsens or improves. In the typical case, the course fluctuates up and down over the long run. Sometimes it is more severe, sometimes it lessens. For some it may go away for weeks, months, or years as mysteriously as it came. But all too frequently, it later returns, and the natural progression of stages begins anew.

Stages do not always follow exactly the order outlined above; the hypochondriac stage and the depression particularly may occur earlier or later. But in general there is some tendency for the disease to progress in its severe form through all seven stages one way or another. In the great majority of cases the first events are the spontaneous attacks, which lead to progressive phobic avoidance and increasing depression or de-moralisation.

Much of the confusion in describing and diagnosing this condition in the past has sprung from viewing this one process at many different points in time. The problems, seen at each point, were given separate diagnostic labels. In effect, a different disorder name was attached to each stage, as if each was a distinct disorder. In contrast, a long-range view, as presented here, reveals one disorder progressing through its various stages. This view is simpler. It makes more common sense; and as we will see in the treatment section, it helps guide us better toward an efficient and successful treatment.

Diseased Nature oftentimes breaks forth
In strange eruptions.

SHAKESPEARE, *Henry IV: Part I*

11. *OTHER COMPLICATIONS*

Traveling the road of this disease, victims may be ambushed by additional catastrophes. The anxiety disease can destroy sleep, ruin sex life, and disrupt appetite. It even drives some people to drink.

SLEEP

A variety of changes in sleep pattern have been reported by patients with this condition. One involves difficulty in falling asleep (known technically as initial or early insomnia), and/or waking up in the middle part of the night from restless and disturbed sleep (middle insomnia). Victims may take up to an hour or more to fall asleep, when it only took a few minutes before. Although they may feel weak and tired during the day, when they lie down to sleep, the switch-off mechanism is faulty. Then a few hours later they awaken, feel restless,

66

toss and turn, visit the bathroom, listen to the late-night talk shows on the radio, and fall asleep only to reawaken an hour or two afterward. This is not only irritating but drains them, so they cannot function well the following day.

Another form of insomnia involves waking in the early morning some hours before the scheduled time, although this disorder occurs only rarely. The early morning wakening is often associated with an inability to get back to sleep until it is time to get up. It is frequently accompanied by an inner restlessness and agitation, "like a motor in my middle that keeps turning over and won't turn off," said one patient. This sensation is worse in the morning hours and fades as the day progresses. So-called early morning awakening (terminal insomnia) is most frequently seen in the condition known as endogenous depression, or major depressive illness. This is a severe form of depression associated with biochemical changes in the central nervous system. Like endogenous anxiety, this endogenous depressive illness can be treated effectively. When the symptom occurs to any significant degree in the anxiety disease, it is usually associated with severe depression.

A third sleep-related symptom also seems peculiar to this disorder. It is called night panic, or pavor nocturnus in medical terminology. A patient may be fully asleep. Then suddenly he or she wakes up in a state of terror, overcome by panic. Most frequently, shortness of breath or racing of the heart is associated with this problem; it is often accompanied by a sensation of dying. At times nightmares occur that are frightening. Some of these images, and often recurrent ones, may be associated with the night panics.

The last common sleep problem frequently found is excessive sleeping. There may be a feeling of weakness, tiredness, and fatigue that persists and yet is not relieved by sleep. People with this symptom will wake up feeling just as fatigued and tired as when they went to bed. They may find themselves sleeping ten to fourteen hours a night; it is as if their sleep does not let the body recover and regain its strength in the normal way. Such excessive daytime fatigue is often called neurasthenia in the medical literature, and many books were written about it during the nineteenth century.

Patients may go through phases of these various sleep disturbances during the course of their illness.

SEXUAL ANXIETY

Nicole began having spells in her mid-twenties and panic attacks at the age of twenty-eight. She had always enjoyed her sexual life, and as her condition progressed, it was the one thing that was a solace to her. During a week when she had had attacks that were more frequent and intense than usual, the confidence she had in her sexuality, which had seemed to grow with the years and experience, started to erode. One night after a bout of particularly protracted and pleasurable sex with her husband, she noticed that she was breathing faster than usual, her heart was racing, she felt hot and flushed, and she had broken out in a sweat. She suddenly realized that these signs of sexual arousal—letting her body go and giving up a sense of control—were uncomfortably like the symptoms of panic attack. She started to gasp for air, her heart wouldn't slow down, she couldn't regain control. Panic came over her. She thought she would actually die.

For weeks afterward this experience replayed itself over and over in Nicole's mind. With each succeeding sexual encounter, she turned her arousal off at an earlier point. She kept fearing she would lose control, so she couldn't give herself up completely. Part of her mind remained detached, outside her, watching the whole thing, "protecting" her.

She began to interpret every expression of arousal as the start of a spell or panic attack. There were so many similarities. She even began to worry about her husband—what if he had a panic attack and lost control? Slowly, she started to avoid sex more and more. It became less pleasurable. She thought of it as a form of mental castration that took you from the inside.

What happened to Nicole was that panic and orgasm became so associated in her mind that she feared getting a repeat panic attack with each subsequent orgasm. Then, when an attack occurred, this confirmed her worst fears. The only obvious solution was not to allow herself to experience arousal beyond a certain point. Indeed, the less sexual activity she had, the less likelihood of any panic. So her sexual life deteriorated. The difficulties that sprung from this problem led her finally to seek treatment for her underlying condition.

Many patients have not run into this misfortune, but it is

probably a more common problem than we know. As the sexual activity and performance is disrupted, the sexual interest is also soon lost. Men are not immune to this problem, either, which can lead to erection failure or more rapid or retarded ejaculation. The result is that soon sexual interest and drive also diminish.

APPETITE

Not only sexual appetite but appetite for food can also fall prey to terror. As in the case of sleep, it can bring about changes that seem to be at opposite ends of the spectrum. Some people lose their appetite and weight. Others, who find the eating of food to be tranquilizing, overeat, especially when anxious, and therefore gain weight. Maria, for example, worried about choking on food and feared swallowing; she often felt hungry but feared the process of eating. It was easier to avoid food. Some weight loss was inevitable. At times, revulsion to food may become marked, and nausea and even repeated episodes of vomiting occur.

Some patients have been erroneously diagnosed as having anorexia nervosa, a condition that is different from the anxiety disease. Sometimes the feeling of anxiety is associated with an awareness of emptiness in the stomach—a gnawing or a sensation of fainting occurs. Some people find that eating seems to relieve these sensations. Over time, they fall into the habit of treating this symptom earlier and more frequently with food. Even the lack of fullness may trigger them to fear that the faint feeling will recur, so keeping it away constantly with food becomes routine. With effective treatment, these extremes of appetite behavior usually revert to the pattern that existed before the condition started.

ALCOHOL AND DRUG ABUSE

Approximately one in five panic victims abuses alcohol or drugs at some point in the course of his or her illness, in an attempt to control the symptoms. Many have found that alcohol is effective in giving short-term and at least partial relief from the suffering. Unfortunately, alcohol exerts its beneficial action only for a few hours and meantime takes its toll. When it wears off, a rebound of the suppressed symptoms occurs, and the drinker feels more anxious and panicky, which drives him to more drink.

There are probably people who are considered alcoholic who only drink to control their anxiety disease. When this is treated successfully, their strong urge to drink lessens. The alcoholism is really only secondary to the anxiety disease, a complication of it. This is probably true of a minority of all alcoholics, but considering the extent of alcoholism, that could translate into a large number of people.

Similarly, there are many drugs that, like alcohol, exert a partial or brief effect in reducing the symptoms. Like pacifiers, they take the edge off the condition without really controlling it. These include barbiturates and sleeping tablets. It is common knowledge among experts in the field, and especially among the patients who take them, that such drugs do not stop spontaneous panic attacks. But because patients often feel some reduction of tension and anxiety when they use them, they feel a little more will help more and eventually block the panic attacks. In cases of severe anxiety and panic, there is therefore an inbuilt urge to take more of these drugs to control the suffering. Some people dismiss this as a form of addiction. But it is not that simple. It is more that these terrified people desperately want relief; they are seeking more of anything that offers them that hope.

> 'Tis not a life,
> 'Tis but a piece of childhood thrown away.
>
> BEAUMONT AND FLETCHER, *Philaster*

12. *FRIGHTENED CHILDREN*

There are few things in the world that inspire action as readily as the sight of a frightened child. Perhaps it is simply a fundamental drive of life to want to rescue the young from fear, from tears, from terror and sadness. It is usually easy to soothe, calm, and reassure—the stress is so clear, and the adult is perceived as a powerful protector, one who can overcome or provide relief from these stresses.

But what if a child is chronically frightened? The stress is not apparent. The adult does not understand the nature of the fear and the child is at a loss to explain it. When he tries, those around do not quite understand. Their reassurances miss the point of the communication. If so, how can they possibly help? The child does not have the words or images to convey it. There are no bruises, cuts, wounds, or broken bones that are obvious manifestations of this inner injury. It is an inner fear that must be suffered alone—and is all the more frightening for that reason.

Zoe might have been any pretty little girl. She had large brown eyes, long dark eyelashes, and a little tilt to her head, the kind that painters portray to evoke sympathy. You were drawn to her. But Zoe was different from her friends. She fainted a lot in school, and often had stomach cramps that kept her out of school. It seemed as if she was always on a visit to one doctor or another with this or that complaint. She had had so many X-rays in the course of her many medical work-ups that her parents began to worry about the effects accumulating and harming her later in life.

At first they thought she had petit mal epilepsy, which is not uncommon in children. But nothing abnormal showed up on her EEG, the brain-wave test for epilepsy. In fact, nothing was found to be abnormal in any of her checkups. The doctors suggested that Zoe was just a nervous child, that perhaps there were problems at school or at home.

Her parents had several conferences with the teachers at school, but nothing unusual was going on apart from her obvious symptoms. The teachers could see that she was getting more phobic of school and that concerned them. The parents wondered whether there was something wrong with their family life, though they had never worried about that before. Their two other children were well adjusted. Perhaps they had done something wrong in bringing up Zoe. They examined the many instances and lived through the usual doubts. But again, in the final analysis, there seemed to be nothing unusually wrong there. Hadn't other children, and they themselves as children, lived through the same experiences?

When they asked Zoe if she could explain what was wrong, she would simply describe her spells, one symptom or another. As they persisted with their relentless questions, she would often make up things that had happened to her. They seemed to want that. She wanted their protection and security, and it seemed like a fair exchange. Each night she feared she would die in her sleep and had to straighten everything out with God. She felt God was the only one who would understand.

*   *   *

Zoe's case is quite typical. While it is unusual for the disease to start before the teens, it certainly does occur. There are few schools that don't have at least one symptomatic, phobic-anxious child. So children are not immune from the anxiety disease.

As with many childhood problems, the manifestations are often simple. Children usually concentrate on their physical symptoms: they describe literally how the spells affect their bodies and where. While they are concentrating on their body reactions, adults notice their avoidance behaviors. These children may be especially frightened of separation, and this persists both more intensely and beyond the phase when most of their peers have long outgrown it. School phobias are a particularly common manifestation of such separation anxiety. Their fears and avoidance may extend to anything, as in adults, and their fears are likely to be multiple and diverse.

Some children go through phases like this, and then as mysteriously as it came, the condition goes into remission. The symptoms may come and go in extended phases, only to appear in full bloom in the late teens or early twenties. Many adults with panic attacks and agoraphobia describe having such phases as children. Mothers treated and recovered from anxiety disease often bring one of their children for early consultation, fearing they will have or are already showing signs of the disease. Parents should not feel guilty or blame themselves. They usually did the best they could given all the circumstances.

Many parents wish they could have done more or done something differently. But, in general, it is fair to say that doing things differently might have made no difference in the long run. Child-rearing practices do not cause the anxiety disease, any more than they cause other childhood diseases. Stress, of course, can be an important aggravator, as it is with many illnesses.

Above all, when parents discover that their child has the disease, they need to find someone who is truly skilled and experienced in treating this disorder.

Part Three _____
CAUSES
_____

There is no question that the problem of
anxiety is a nodal point at which the most
various and important questions converge,
a riddle whose solution would be bound
to throw a flood of light on our whole
mental existence.

SIGMUND FREUD, *Introductory
Lectures on Psychoanalysis*

Part Three

CAUSES

> *What is laid down, ordered, factual, is never enough to embrace the whole truth; life always spills over the rim of every cup.*

> BORIS PASTERNAK

13. *AN INTERPLAY OF THREE FORCES*

The eight-month-old baby reached out her soft, plump hand, patted her mother's face, and pulled it close. There was radiant delight and trust in the child's face, and her mother, too, was absorbed in their shared pleasure in each other. Then the child buried her head in the comforting curve of her mother's shoulder. The visual image of that fleeting moment fixed itself in Maria's memory and would later haunt her.

The mother was a friend of Maria's who had come with her baby to visit. At first Maria had been happy to see them. She wanted to be able to share in some of the pleasures of motherhood. But now the sight of the baby nestled so comfortably in her friend's arms irritated her. Something in her wanted to disrupt the scene. Competitive, jealous thoughts raced across her mind, and she hated herself for them. She wished her friend would leave so that the painful emotions would go away also. Maria tried to be casual, but there was a

77

choking sensation in her throat and she was afraid she was going to cry. She had dreamed so often of holding her own baby, of loving and caring for it as her friend did. But at this moment she feared it would never be.

Her anxiety disease appeared to be an insurmountable wall separating her from normal motherhood. No suitable man would ever want to marry her in her condition, she worried, or father her child. And if she did marry, it would not be right for her to have children, anyway. How could she manage a pregnancy and delivery when the simple matters of daily life were so often overwhelming? How could she raise a child? Wouldn't it be traumatic for a child to see her in one of her panic attacks? Would the child learn from her to be fearful? Perhaps she would condition the child by her own behavior to be like her. In Maria's moments of optimism, she thought it would be possible not to pass it on if she mothered the child well. However, if this condition was genetically inherited, then it could be passed on despite her best efforts. Her baby could be afflicted no matter how she mothered it. Maria's mind was a jumble of conflicting fears and hopes. She wished she understood better what caused the condition. Was it nature or nurture or both, and if both, how did they interact?

HISTORICAL MODELS OF ANXIETY

In understanding abnormal anxiety, man has used three models. Initially, he attributed abnormal anxiety to environmental events. Perhaps the phase of the moon, the work of an evil spirit, or the stress of overwhelming life events explained it.

Sigmund Freud, who had symptoms of anxiety disease himself, although not in a severe form, worried a great deal about his spells and had many medical evaluations for them. But nothing of a serious medical nature could be found wrong with him. He was told that his symptoms were "nervous" in origin. Freud was not satisfied that the environmental stress model fully explained his symptoms, since many details did not fit and this model did not reflect his own reality accurately enough. In his quest for a fuller explanation, he searched psychologically, specifically into his own dreams. He built an elaborate model based on the psychology of the mind and the role of internal conflicts in causing and maintaining anxiety. This model has preoccupied everyone studying anxiety for most of this century. But the psychological model also has its limitations. It, too, seemed only part of the story.

Many eminent physicians have suggested that there may be a physical basis for abnormal anxiety. But nothing could ever be found that was wrong physically, largely because the brain has been the last gland in the body to be studied intensively by scientists. The technology to examine and investigate its inner workings was not available until recently and is still evolving. But evidence is now accumulating that there may be a physical cause of the anxiety disease. This development is still in the early stages of investigation. The physical defects appear crucial, even central to the whole problem. But the physical model, too, is not the whole answer, though it may contain the significant and greater part of it.

Each of these models—the environmental stress model, the psychological model, and the physical model—contributed something to our overall understanding of abnormal anxiety. But each had its limitations. In the following pages, we shall attempt to build an even better model.

A NEW MODEL: THE INTERPLAY OF THREE FORCES

Models in science are attempts to bring order and lucidity to the variety of observations. A good model is a description that accurately reflects reality. So, good science is accurate description: it is a description of events and especially their interplay. The better the science, the more accurate the description. Sometimes science may describe things that appear to be obvious to the lay person. But the technique of making these descriptions extraordinarily precise is what the work of a scientist is all about.

A good model of the anxiety disease should demonstrate how the spontaneous panic attacks, the many spells, and the phobias are related, in a way that makes sense and accurately reflects reality. Such a model should describe the mechanisms underlying the development of the diverse symptoms and phobias. It should also define how the sequence occurs. For only by describing how the sequence occurs can we predict more about the disease and learn to control it more effectively.

The model outlined in this book is based on the interplay of three forces: biological, psychological conditioning, and stress. These forces are the threads connecting the stages described earlier. Understanding them helps us to understand the natural progression of the disorder and the interplay of various symptoms and complications. Together with a longitudinal view of the disease passing through its seven stages, these three forces and their interplay paint a richer picture of how the many parts are woven together.

But we must always keep in mind that this model is still only a reflection of real life. Like all models in science, it too will be improved and refined. In this way, we move closer to a fuller understanding of the disease and its eventual conquest.

> *The expectation that every neurotic phenomenon can be cured may, I suspect, be derived from the layman's belief that the neuroses are something quite unnecessary which have no right whatever to exist. Whereas in fact they are severe, constitutionally fixed illnesses, which rarely restrict themselves to only a few attacks but persist as a rule over long periods or throughout life.*
>
> SIGMUND FREUD, *New Introductory Lectures on Psychoanalysis*

14. *FORCE 1: BIOLOGICAL*

Maria knew that many women have careers and choose not to have children, but she was well aware that they had a choice. Even if she chose not to have a child, Maria wanted to feel her options, too, were open. She felt her condition, particularly her not understanding it fully, severely restricted her choices. She felt she was cut off from something, felt like something was missing, and felt empty as a result, particularly when she was around her friends who were married and had children and seemed fulfilled in some way. It was as if other women could have something she could not have and this would condemn her to a certain loneliness. As her condition worsened new fears grew, distancing her further from the idea of having a child. She was afraid of a pregnancy—a growing life inside her that would be completely dependent on her and from which she couldn't escape. She feared having a child that was defective either emotionally or physically. She feared the possibility of passing on her condition in

81

some genetic way. Was it genetically inherited? What was known about its medical cause? She needed to find answers to these questions so that she could resolve some of the many confused and conflicting feelings she had about her future.

The central force in the anxiety disease appears to be a physical one. The proposed model suggests that at the center of this disease, feeding it like a spring, is a biological and probably a biochemical disorder.

What triggered the idea that something could be wrong physically or biochemically? For one thing, the patients themselves have so persistently felt that it had to be. This whole problem was outside the range of normal functioning and anxiety experience. It was bizarre. They were so often at a loss to explain it to themselves in any other way. And to medical scientists, there were other clues that the disorder might be physically based.

First, there was evidence suggesting that vulnerability to the disorder may be genetically inherited. Many patients told their physicians that other members of their families had similar symptoms. Statistical studies were done on the prevalence of the disorder among the relatives of affected people. It was found that those who had a close relative with the condition were more likely to develop it than those who did not. This finding was strong enough for it to be highly unlikely that it was due to chance alone. It also seemed that the closer the biological relationship to the affected person, the greater the likelihood of developing the disorder. Special mathematical techniques were used to analyze the family trees of affected families. The evidence suggested that the proneness to this disorder fit closely, though not perfectly, with a dominant-gene inheritance pattern. This inheritance pattern would allow it to be passed down by one parent, and would not require it to be inherited from both sides of the family.

The anxiety disease has also been shown to be strongly associated with the presence of a heart condition known as mitral valve prolapse. Among patients with panic attacks, approximately one in every three also has this disorder, which involves a floppy mitral valve in the heart. This floppy mitral valve is believed to be inherited through a dominant gene. The disorder is not usually considered a serious heart problem. Although no one yet fully understands the relationship between the two conditions, the frequent coexistence of the anxiety disease with the inherited mitral valve prolapse lends some further support to the idea that there is some genetic vulnerability to the anxiety disease.

Currently, twins with the condition are being studied. The findings suggest that there is a greater tendency for both twins to have the anxiety disease if they are identical than if they are nonidentical twins. Twin studies like these are frequently used to sort out the relative contributions of environmental (stress and learning) factors from genetic factors. If a disease is learned or due to an environmental stress, then growing up at the same time in the same family, exposed to the same environment, should result in both twins having it equally, whether they are identical or not. On the other hand, if it is mainly genetic, you would expect both of the identical twins who have an identical genetic makeup to have it together. The findings in the twin study suggest that genetic inheritance forces tend to outweigh the effects of the environment in their overall contribution to the disorder.

It is possible that such a genetic weakness could give rise to biochemical abnormalities, and that these in turn could lead to the symptoms the victim feels physically. What are the precise, biochemical abnormalities in this disease? No one knows yet with certainty. However, this is an exciting time in the field since several teams of individuals in major medical schools are now trying to uncover the mystery. And the reason for the excitement is that there are some good leads. The question among these medical scientists is no longer whether or not there is a biochemical or metabolic abnormality. The question is rather, how can we pin it down and describe it as thoroughly as possible?

The best guesses so far involve certain nerve endings and receptors in the central nervous system which produce and receive chemical messengers that stimulate and excite the brain. These nerve endings manufacture naturally occurring stimulants called catecholamines. It is believed that in the anxiety disease, the nerve endings are overfiring. They are working too hard, overproducing these stimulants and perhaps others.

At the same time there are nerve endings and receptors that have the opposite effect: they produce naturally occurring tranquilizers, called inhibitory neurotransmitters, that inhibit, calm down, and dampen the nerve firing of the brain. It appears that the neurotransmitters or the receptors may be deficient, either in quality or quantity.

Why are they deficient? Several other substances regulate the firing of the nerves, acting like accelerators or brakes on the firing process. These substances include prostaglandins, which are local regulators, and ions, especially calcium ions, which flow across cell membranes. Enzymes regulate how fast these substances are produced and destroyed in the nerve endings. There is some evidence suggesting that all of these substances may be involved in some way in the malfunctions that produce the anxiety disease. A chain of events apparently runs from the inherited gene or genes through the cell nucleus to the cell membrane to the nerve ending and the chemicals it uses, involving some or all of the above mechanisms. As the solution unfolds, undoubtedly other neuropeptides and neurotransmitters will be identified that play a role in that chain. The picture will become clearer as each piece is added. The important point is that we already have some framework on which to build; increasingly, the technology is available to search deeper.

Another clue to the physical nature of the disease was discovered by Dr. Mandel Cohen and his colleagues at Harvard Medical School. In the 1940s, they found that some patients with severe anxiety often had intolerance to over-exercising. That is, when they were forced to exercise for a long time on a treadmill, for example, their symptoms got worse. One of the main by-products of muscle activity is lactate. In the search for clues, the lactate level in the blood of these patients was found to be elevated. It seems that for some reason these people either overproduced lactate and were unable to handle it chemically, or their bodies were abnormally sensitive to it.

In 1966 a doctor named Ferris Pitts found that giving an intravenous infusion of sodium lactate to victims of this disease brought on spells and panic just like their original symptoms. It is possible to turn the condition on simply by injecting this substance, which is produced in everyone's body in response to exercise. If you give sodium lactate to normal individuals, nothing happens; with anxiety disease victims, turning off the lactate infusions stops the symptoms.

Then it was found that putting calcium ions in the infusion reduced the intensity of attacks. Later still, three families of drugs—known as the MAO inhibitors, the tricyclics, and the triazolobenzodiazepine (alprazolam)—attenuated the panic and spells induced by lactate. A patient who was sensitive to lactate could be given a lactate infusion after treatment with any of these drugs and not develop the panic attacks. The drugs change the patients' metabolism in such a way that they are not abnormally sensitive to lactate, and so respond once again more like normal people. In 1984 a team at the Washington University School of Medicine used a new technology called positron emission tomography (PET) scanning to get a picture of the blood flow in various regions of the brain during a lactate induced anxiety attack. They found an abnormal left-right blood flow asymmetry in a small region of the brain called the parahippocampal gyrus, a region that is believed to play an important role in the expression of emotion and in fear. This was the first time that a discrete brain abnormality had been identified in this anxiety disease. What had previously only been felt by a patient could now be seen, photographed, and pinpointed objectively.

Since these initial discoveries, other drugs have been found to have the same panic-inducing effects as lactate; these include substances like isoproterenol and yohimbine. The drugs that turn the condition on have some effects in common with the mechanisms of the disease, just as those that turn off the symptoms must all have some shared qualities that have opposite effects on the disease. When these precise effects are understood, they will provide valuable clues to the exact cause of the disease.

In a series of studies in the 1970s, Dr. Eugene Redmond of Yale demonstrated the effect certain parts of the brain have on the behavior and emotional reaction to fear. He implanted an electrode in a small center of the lower brain—known as the locus coeruleus—of stumptailed monkeys. When this electrode was stimulated electrically, the monkeys behaved as if they were panicked, anxious, fearful, or in impending danger. In contrast, damaging this small brain center in the monkeys had the opposite effect: the monkeys without a functioning locus coeruleus showed an absence of emotional response to threats, and they were without apparent fear of approaching humans or dominant monkeys. Socially, they were more aggressive, and they moved around in their cage much more than before and more than normal monkeys. Since the locus coeruleus has the highest density of norepinephrine-containing neurons in the central nervous system, Redmond proposed from these studies that panic and fear result from a hyperactivity of these neurons in the brain.

The fact that anxiety and fear could be switched on and off in this fashion conveys the idea of how physical this problem could be. The site of the locus coeruleus is one of the most permeable areas of the brain and in this way one of the most sensitive areas to local metabolic changes. When the particular biochemical changes associated with the anxiety disease occur, this part of the brain may be the most sensitive to the changes and is stimulated to produce its characteristic fear reaction.

Whatever biological disturbance contributes to the anxiety disease, the effect is that at a rate of approximately two to four times per week patients have sudden discharges of spontaneous anxiety attacks and spells that have a devastating psychological impact. Anxiety and fear are experienced as a result of these attacks. The central metabolic core, fed by the apparent biochemical abnormality, fires off symptoms throughout the patient's body. In the following chapters we will see the result of this mechanism and how it in turn sets other forces in motion.

> *Experiment alone crowns the efforts of medicine. . . . Observation discloses . . . numerous phenomena existing side by side and interconnected now profoundly, now indirectly or accidentally. . . .*
>
> *Experiment, as it were, takes the phenomena in hand, sets in motion now one of them, and another, and then by means of artificial, simplified combinations, discovers the actual connection between the phenomena.*
>
> IVAN PAVLOV, *Experimental Psychology and Other Essays*

15. FORCE 2: CONDITIONING

It must have been the distant, reflective expression on Maria's face that prompted her friend to give Maria the baby to hold. Maria knew the gesture was meant kindly, but for her it was also a challenge, a test of how well she could mother a child. With the baby in her arms she felt on trial. Part of her mind was standing back, watching and judging her. Because of all these feelings, she couldn't act naturally, and as children do, the infant quickly sensed her discomfort and began to push away fearfully, and then began to cry. Maria tried hard to be comforting, but forcing herself on the child made matters worse, so her friend took the child back and patiently comforted her. Her friend's success in calming the child only added to Maria's feeling that she had failed. The incident had confirmed her fear that a baby could detect her feelings and would respond to them with fear and anxiety and reject her. If that happened often enough, thought Maria, she would surely train her child to be fearful. She didn't know exactly how people learned phobias, although she recalled reading articles about it and remembered from her college psychology courses that conditioning was involved. She herself, though, couldn't recall learning her fears from anyone. If learning was a factor in the cause of her phobias, how did it work and how was it related to the biochemical disease aspects of the disorder?

The second major force in the anxiety disease involves various kinds of conditioning. The mind reacts to spontaneous anxiety attacks by trying to avoid them. Such self-preservation mechanisms, although they protect in one way, in other ways may restrict, disable, and depress the victim still further. This sets up a battle between self-preservation on the one side and progressive disability on the other. The stronger the self-preservation reaction, the worse the disability usually becomes.

Overcoming the disability psychologically involves taking risks, not giving in to self-protection totally; for this reason, it can be somewhat threatening and frightening. Let us look at the way these spontaneous anxiety attacks can bring about the effects they do, and while protecting in one way make the anxiety and phobias worse in another.

MECHANISM 1: CLASSICAL CONDITIONING

Any miscellaneous event can be associated by the mind with a specific response. The effects that the spontaneous anxiety attacks and spells have on an individual are immediate and unmistakable: they produce symptoms throughout the body and an anxiety/fear response. And just as Pavlov's dogs learned to associate bells with food, and therefore salivated at the sound of bells even when no food was present, so any miscellaneous event that happens to be going on when someone has a spontaneous anxiety attack can acquire the ability to bring on the anxiety/fear reaction, even when no spontaneous anxiety attack occurs. A person who was riding in a subway train when an attack occurred will have a physical reaction when next in a subway that was never associated with the subway before. From then on the subway brings on an anxiety/fear response, a flight response (wanting to run away), and eventually a phobia (a wish to avoid the subway in the future). Usually this kind of association between the spontaneous attacks and the miscellaneous events occurs several times before a phobia is established. However, if the spontaneous attack is intense enough, it may only need to happen once to produce a phobia.

The speed with which people with this disease sometimes acquire phobias raises the question of whether the biochemical changes in the nervous system associated with spontaneous attacks somehow chemically speed up such rapid learning of new phobias.

With time, as the spontaneous attacks occur in a variety of settings, a greater number of settings become new triggers for phobic anxiety and avoidance behavior. It should be stressed that there need not be any relationship between a particular miscellaneous event and the original spontaneous attack for it to become the focus of a new phobia. A great many things can become stimuli for anxiety without their ever having any prior association to anxiety. We have seen everything from ice cream cones to spaghetti to lazing on the beach in the sun become the focus of a phobia in this way.

The relationship between this learning by association and the physical causes of the anxiety disease is illustrated in Figure 4. Anxiety, fear, and its symptoms are first fired off from within the individual by the spontaneous attack because of the biochemical core abnormality. Then, with time, miscellaneous situations in the environment also acquire by association the ability to bring on anxiety, fear, and phobias. At any point along the course of the disorder, the spontaneous attacks may stop. But the phobias triggered by the miscellaneous situations may continue. In addition, by this time the phobias are now fed through other mechanisms we will see shortly, and by repeated avoidance.

After several years of the anxiety disease, patients usually have a combination of spontaneous attacks and of anxiety and phobias that are triggered by these miscellaneous situations. In effect, the anxiety symptoms and phobias are being triggered and fed from inside the patient by the disease, and from outside by the miscellaneous situations. However, patients describe these two anxiety experiences as different. One is the disease-based spontaneous attack. The second is the

Figure 4. Sources of symptom induction

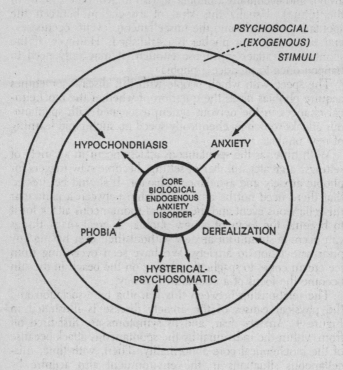

anticipatory anxiety to the miscellaneous situation, which develops from its association with the original spontaneous attack.

When the anxiety disease has progressed for a number of years, spontaneous attacks usually make up from 20 to 50 percent of the anxiety experiences, occurring on average two to four times per week. The rest are anticipatory anxieties due to a fear of the miscellaneous situations.

This model makes clear a number of points: a patient with spontaneous attacks may learn to be phobic of any miscellaneous situations. And the longer he has the anxiety disease, and the more intense and frequent the spontaneous attacks, the more phobias he will acquire.

MECHANISM 2: THE RIPPLE EFFECT

Picture a drop falling onto the surface of a perfectly smooth pond. When the drop hits the surface, it will have its greatest effect at the point of impact; however, ripples quickly spread out to more distant parts of the pond, and these ripples get weaker as they spread. It is clear that the effects of a drop are felt well beyond its original point of impact.

Phobias and anxiety spread in a similar way. This ripple effect phenomenon is referred to as stimulus generalization. For example, suppose a patient had a spontaneous attack while visiting with a neighbor to see her new cat. After that, she phobically avoided all cats. She then feared any furry animals or even wearing furry clothes herself. Finally, she would experience discomfort even seeing a stranger wearing a fur coat. The original trigger for fear spread first to items that were related to it; then, over time, it spread to a wider field, to embrace more distantly related items that became new triggers for anxiety. The more distant triggers were not as powerful in bringing anxiety as the central source.

Studies have shown that this stimulus generalization is greater when someone is unaware of what is triggering the anxiety. Since patients with the anxiety disease complain of sudden spontaneous anxiety attacks that occur unprovoked and without warning, we would expect their anxiety to spread out like ripples and to embrace new phobias more rapidly.

In this way, anxiety and phobic avoidance can be controlled by complex combinations of internal and external triggers. They may be either closely related to or remote from the central unconditioned stimuli. The phobia may spread to other situations and things that are similar physically or that sound verbally similar; they even spread to situations that are unique to each individual, because everyone's association network is unique. The fact that new stimuli can bring on anxiety and phobias in the several ways discussed in this chapter adds to the complexity of the process. It also complicates attempts to unravel the phobic disorder by psychological or behavioral means alone.

MECHANISM 3: REWARD LEARNING
AND AVOIDANCE TRAINING

B. F. Skinner, a Harvard professor of psychology and one of the great scientists of the twentieth century, undertook a series of studies aimed at showing how behavior could be influenced. Using pigeons, he tried systematically to catalogue the many ways in which he could increase the frequency and intensity of their pecking. Of the ways he found, three are now well known.

The first is called reward learning. Skinner gave the pigeon a reward (a little food pellet) when he wanted to increase one kind of pecking. For example, if the pigeon pecked to the right side, a pellet immediately appeared. Pecking in any other direction was not rewarded. After a while, the pigeon pecked more to the right side than it would normally do. From this experiment Skinner described a principle with general applications to learning. Any behavior, he found, increases in frequency and strength when it is followed by a reinforcement.

There are many ways in which this principle may influence anxiety and phobic symptoms. One obvious one is that giving a patient with these symptoms financial disability benefits may actually reinforce the symptoms. It may be compassionate and humanly laudable to do so, but this should not be confused with the fact that in so doing the behavior is reinforced.

The other two well-known mechanisms of reinforcement described by Skinner are escape training and avoidance training. In escape training, the relief of escaping from something unpleasant, like an electric shock, is a positive reward. In the anxiety disease, running away from a situation in which a spontaneous attack occurred makes it more likely that the person will run away next time, perhaps sooner and with greater haste. This is because as the person is running away, the anxiety intensity usually lessens, since attacks are usually time-limited, and running away becomes associated with relief from anxiety. In avoidance learning, any behavior that seems to prevent the unpleasant experience from appearing in effect becomes a reward. In the case of the anxiety disease, avoidance of phobic situations actually increases the strength of the phobia itself.

"Security blankets" are a curious spin-off of these kinds of conditioning. When patients talk about their "security blankets," it is often apologetically or with a little embarrassment. Just as they associate certain situations with fear, patients come to associate certain things with relief. Many patients with this disorder create their own special security blankets to diminish the anxiety, to prevent an attack, or to somehow cope with the experience; these are often helpful in small ways to individual patients.

One lady needed to prepare a whole well-balanced meal the day before taking even a short trip of ten miles or more. It had to be carefully packed in containers and flasks for the journey. She almost never ate these meals, but took them along "just in case." She thought the right food might help her spells of faintness. Another took a flask of vodka everywhere in her car and purse. The same unopened flask of vodka was still with her after five years. A third felt fearful without driving with her dog at her side. And a fourth brought a weather radio as a security against being overtaken and cut off by a storm. Carrying around old, out-of-date medications is reassuring to some people. One woman was too fearful to drive far from home lest she should get stranded and be unable to find help. After she had a car telephone installed, she functioned quite well in driving. Then one week the system in her car was out of order, and she again became too phobic to drive without it.

Security blankets are always very individual possessions. They may appear odd to others, but they can help people cope better. For some, in the midst of a life of terror, it may be the only security they can find. One patient summed it up when she said, "It may be odd, but it's all I've got."

MECHANISM 4:
CIVIL WAR WITHIN THE BODY

One part of the body may turn on another part, even when the two didn't influence each other previously to any significant degree. An intelligent, observant patient tried to find some threads that would explain why so many of his spells and spontaneous attacks came on for no good reason: while watching the closing moments of an exciting football game on TV, his heart sped up, he became panicky and had a series of other symptoms. This annoyed him since it took him away from his game. The same thing occurred when he ran upstairs, exercised, had vigorous sexual relations, laughed too much, or got too delighted about anything.

After keeping records on himself over a period of time, he found a connection between his heart racing and the anxiety symptoms that always seemed to follow. What appeared to be happening was that on several occasions after his heart was running fast for whatever reason, he had a spontaneous attack of anxiety and spells. This probably happened several times. By association, the racing of the heart acquired the ability to bring on anxiety and symptoms elsewhere, even when there was nothing to be anxious about. In effect, an organ in the body had acquired the ability to bring on anxiety and fear even though it had never done so before and was not intended to function that way. Not only can anxiety bring on all kinds of physical changes in various parts of the body; equally, an organ or a body function may become a trigger for anxiety or a spell.

This so-called interoceptive conditioning takes longer to develop than conditioning to external stimuli. However, once it gets a hold, it is often more fixed and difficult to reverse. This may help explain why so many apparently unrelated symptoms could set each other off in various combinations, and why a patient often cannot make sense of these patterns.

MECHANISM 5: HIGH AROUSAL REGRESSION

The above mechanisms explain some but not all of the ways phobias can develop. Because many of the panic attacks in the anxiety disease are spontaneous, we would expect a random selection of phobias. However, in those patients who have the chronic, severe form of the disease, there seems to be a pattern to the several clusters of phobias acquired:

- fears of going insane, of losing control or being overwhelmed by inner sensations,
- separation anxiety fears,
- social fears,
- fears of body illness, injury, or health worries.

Why do so many patients acquire these particular phobic clusters?

PETROVA'S NEUROTIC DOGS

In one series of studies, young puppies were first conditioned by Petrova, a pupil of Pavlov, to become phobic to noxious stimuli. The pups were then treated so that they lost these phobias. Much later, when the dogs became adults, they were made experimentally neurotic and put into a high stress arousal state. In this high arousal state, the phobic avoidance to noxious stimuli they had had as pups returned. This and other animal experiments demonstrate that when an animal is stressed and the usual coping mechanism is prevented or fails, there is regression to earlier coping strategies. In other words, a high arousal state in adult life could reactivate fearful behavior that was present at an earlier developmental phase.

The psychoanalytic and developmental psychology literature describes several anxieties said to be typical of childhood. The first of these, sometimes termed *impulse* anxiety, is said to occur when the infant feels overwhelmed by needs and feelings that he is unable to control in his helpless state. A regression to this anxious behavior could reactivate fears of loss of control, and of being overwhelmed by inner sensations.

The second typical anxiety phase that children may experience between the ages of eight months and three years is termed *stranger* anxiety. Regression to this response could be reactivated as social phobias.

The third anxiety phase, seen typically in children between two and four years of age, is known as *separation* anxiety. Regression to this response could reactivate the fears typical of agoraphobics—of being far from home, from points of security, friends, or family, and of being left alone.

At four or five years of age, separation anxiety is said to fade out, to be replaced by fears of injury or body illness. Freud called this fear *castration* anxiety. Regression to these fears would appear in the form of illness or injury phobias and hypochondriasis.

This kind of regression, as a result of the high arousal state produced by unexpected panic attacks, would partially explain the pattern of phobia choice in these patients. There may be some biological mechanism that regulates development through these critical fear periods in children. Humans may be born with a biological predisposition to learn certain phobias, such as those mentioned above, more easily than others. Rhesus monkeys for example are believed to have a biological preparedness that predisposes them to learn and maintain snake phobias more easily than they can be conditioned to fear a flower. It is likely that certain fears could be imprinted more easily than others at different critical stages. The biological core of the anxiety disease may reactivate this imprinting mechanism and biological preparedness. It is quite possible that the biochemical changes occurring during an unexpected anxiety attack are associated with altered production of certain neurochemicals that change normal learning patterns and facilitate more rapid, more complete, and more lasting conditioning of phobias. Although this mechanism is speculative, it is consistent with some experimental data, with some earlier psychological theories (e.g., those of Freud), and with some otherwise puzzling clinical phenomena.

> *Heredity sets limits,*
> *environment decides the exact position within these limits.*
>
> EDWIN CARLETON MACDOWELL

16. *FORCE 3: STRESS*

As Maria's condition worsened, people tried to help her understand and cope with her problem. They would assure her that it was just stress that she needed to put out of her mind. She heard that she should get away from it all so many times she worried she would scream if she heard it again. They thought it was all environmental stress. Adam felt it was stress. The logical solution was to deal with the stress directly—if she could identify it. In her search for solutions, she went to the bookstores and the libraries to read what could be done about it. The material she found all said the same three things in so many dressed-up ways: that her problems were all in her head and caused by stress; that she should identify the exact problem; and that she could overcome it by dealing with it directly.

Maria read several of these books. She never really believed any of them entirely. First, she felt her anxiety and symptoms were not simply a matter of environmental stress. She couldn't identify a good reason either psychologically or environmentally for her having this in the first place. She couldn't identify the problem since the problem *was* having the spells. If she had a problem, it was that it didn't make sense to her. She had tried all the suggestions in the books, but they didn't help very much. She couldn't understand why there were so many books all saying the same thing. Why didn't it work for her? Were other people with this problem so different?

Maria found it hard to believe she was the only one still stuck and not responding. Perhaps the writers ought to spend more time listening to people like her and taking that experience as they found it at face value; they should spend less time writing their own thoughts about it. After all, these people were normal. She had the disease. They depended on her experience to write accurately. Her experience was the raw data for their books—they should listen to her story.

The third major force in the anxiety disease is stress. That environmental stress is a force that causes anxiety has become a truism. The problem is that this explanation seems so obvious, it has come to be accepted as the one and only explanation of anxiety experience. Even if others are acknowledged, its role as the principal force is not questioned. It hardly seems possible that there could be a kind of anxiety that is not mainly stress-related. The one explanation of environmental stress as *the* cause should fit all types. And yet . . . what if there was an anxiety disorder where environmental stress only had a small role to play? Could there be such a condition, in which the contribution of environmental stress was 20 percent, even perhaps 10 percent or less? It seems that in the anxiety disease, the role of environmental stress may have been somewhat exaggerated in the past.

However, in many cases it does play some role. Two kinds of stress are often identified as important troublemakers. There is direct stress, caused by things going wrong in the environment: someone is threatened, loses his job, is faced with divorce or the illness of a child. The soldier on the front line, the victim of rape or robbery, the distraught parent looking for a lost child, the father who has no work and worries how he will feed his family, all are common images of anxiety.

The second variety of anxiety is conflict-related. Two opposing forces are in conflict. Perhaps there is a strong wish to do something and at the same time a strong prohibition saying you can't. Two forces, both equally valid, both needing to be satisfied, may pull in opposite directions. The harried executive forced to choose between two no-win choices is a common example; the young woman torn between two lovers is another.

Environmental stress of all kinds can make any disease worse. It is not so much a cause of disease as an important aggravator. It is neither necessary nor sufficient to cause the disease; but when it is present, it seems to make things worse. It may speed up the onset, intensify the symptoms, weaken the resistance and coping of the patient, accelerate the deterioration, and delay the healing. There are few diseases where its role as an aggravator has not been described. In the anxiety disease its role may be no different, neither more nor less important. Yet, because it can play a significant role, stress cannot be ignored. To do so might spell the difference between success and failure. Just how, and to what extent, it interplays with the other forces certainly demands consideration.

We have considered how a genetic biochemical physical force could set the problem in motion; how psychological mechanisms cope with and at the same time aggravate the problem; and how stress adds fuel to the fires of both, in fanning its first flames or in perpetuating its progress. What is needed is a careful clarification of the role of each, but above all an integrated perspective.

Part Four _____
TREATMENT

Canst thou not minister to a mind diseas'd,
Pluck from the memory a rooted sorrow,
Raze out the written troubles of the brain,
And with some sweet oblivious antidote
Cleanse the stuff'd bosom of that perilous stuff
Which weighs upon the heart?

SHAKESPEARE, *Macbeth*

> *What does it avail you, if of many thorns,*
> *only one be removed?*
>
> HORACE, *Epistolae*

17. THE FOUR TARGETS OF TREATMENT

Although he hadn't called her for some time, Adam was still quite upset over the whole issue. He did care deeply for Maria. But he foresaw a life of emotional complications with her—her fluctuating moods, her many restrictions, her symptoms that always needed medical attention. How could they ever have a family? He saw himself having to play the role of both mother and father. He envisioned endless medical bills, endless complaints, limited joy. Everything he associated with a life of good quality would be denied her. It would also be denied to him because he was associated with her, which would only fuel his resentment of her in the future.

Projected into the future, their life together appeared to offer more thorns than roses. Adam felt guilty about leaving Maria like this; but he also felt he had to resolve these issues in his own mind before restoring their relationship. To do so sooner would renew her hopes and worsen the pain of their eventual breakup. So he stayed away, reviewing the conflict over and over. There seemed to be no satisfactory solution.

Then one day Adam came upon the headline: "Panic Attacks Can Kill" in a science magazine. It reported recent research on a large group of patients with recurrent panic attacks. They were compared with a group of normal people, who in every other way seemed similar except for having no panic attacks. They lived in the same area, led similar lives, had similar age and sex distributions. Following two similar matched groups in this way, one would expect that in the long run they would encounter similar health problems and stresses overall. But the actual findings shocked Adam: The panic attack victims as a group overall died off at a faster rate and at an earlier age than the matched normal group. The conclusion seemed to be that recurrent panic attacks had a harmful effect on longevity.

The symptoms described in these patients were disturbingly similar to Maria's. Adam felt he had to do something, so he went to the local university medical school library. First, there were a number of recent books on anxiety and panic. There were also some computer data bases that had lists of all the papers written on the subject for the past several years; they even gave short descriptions of the main points in each paper, in addition to the exact journal, date, and page numbers where they could be found. One such reservoir of information on computer was called Medline, another Medlars, and there was yet a third, more comprehensive one, compiled by the National Institutes of Health. Later that day, Adam brought home a long computer printout of all the important papers written on the subject in the past three years and abstracts of those papers. He went through it that night and checked off the ones he was most interested in. The librarian then got him reprints of these articles.

Reading them over during the following weeks, he was left with some interesting impressions. There seemed to be just a handful of medical researchers concerned with the subject; the same names kept recurring. There also seemed to be a growing awareness that this was indeed, as Maria had tried to tell him, not just a psychological problem but an actual disease, which could lead to several medical conditions, including the development of high blood pressure, an increased risk of alcoholism and suicide, and an increase in deaths from heart disease in men. But happily it seemed that there was good evidence a few medications were beneficial in treating the disease.

Adam decided to call Maria. He would try to arrange for her to have a consultation with one of these experts. It was such new research that he thought it best Maria should meet someone who dealt with this problem all the time. He began to see that in helping Maria, he was also helping to resolve his own conflict about their relationship. And he was beginning to understand the problem more from Maria's perspective; there was some substance to what she had been trying to tell him.

There is recent evidence that people with panic disorder left untreated and followed over forty years do indeed have an excess mortality when compared to a matched normal control group. It is also fair to say that in capable hands, the great majority of people with the disease can now be treated successfully. There is no longer any need for people to expect they must live with fear—they should be able to live without it. And they should not be satisfied with partial results.

In the past when the disease was ascribed to psychological factors alone, psychological treatments seemed to be a logical choice; but alone, they did not work. Later, when the cause was said to be conditioning, it seemed logical to recommend behavior therapy treatments. But these proved effective only for some of the symptoms of the disease, and sometimes not at all. Alone, they too were not effective enough. Then tranquilizers came into fashion: they took the edge off some of the symptoms, but didn't block the spontaneous panic attacks. Subsequently some other families of medication proved very effective against the spontaneous attacks but did not always completely eliminate the phobias. Depending on which underlying cause each practitioner subscribed to, he or she also had a favorite treatment approach. The treatment seemed to be a logical extension of the diagnosis and understanding of causal mechanisms.

In Part Three, we saw that the causes of the anxiety disease are currently best understood as an interplay of three types of

forces. The first is a genetic-metabolic disease force: a biochemical abnormality that drives the disease. The second are
psychological conditioning factors. And finally a third force—
that of psychosocial or environmental stresses—can aggravate
the problem further. In choosing an effective treatment, it
seems logical to take aim at these three forces and attempt to
control each of them in turn.

So there are four targets of treatment:

1. Control the metabolic core,
2. Overcome the phobias,
3. Deal with the psychosocial environmental stresses,
4. Long-term management.

The first three targets of treatment are directed toward
dealing with each of the three major forces that interplays in
this disorder. The fourth target is directed toward maintaining
the gains achieved with the first three targets. It is also
directed toward teaching the patient about his or her condition and the treatment, so that relapses can be minimized.

In the past, the common course of treatment involved
several steps. First, the patient was treated with psychotherapy, the talking therapy. This was to correct the psychological
causes and deal with them. After several months, if this
failed, he was often sent to a psychologist for behavior therapy
of his phobias, along with training in relaxation methods. If
this was still unsatisfactory, the patient was then treated with
minor tranquilizers.

Recent experience in treating these patients would now
recommend reversing this order of treatment: trying medication first, behavior therapy second, and psychotherapy third.
The core metabolic disease seems to be the anxiety's predominant cause. It is difficult to make satisfactory progress in
treating the disorder without first controlling the metabolic
core with medication. When that has been accomplished, it
is much easier to overcome the phobias with behavior therapy. And sometimes the therapy will even be unnecessary. If
the phobias have been overcome, any remaining environmental stresses or problems that could be aggravating the
disease usually come into sharper focus. The patient's energy,
no longer so tied up in dealing with the disease and its

associated phobias, is now more available to identify and work on these problems. And sometimes there are no environmental problems, in which case psychotherapy is unnecessary.

So the overall strategy for treating the anxious patient is as follows:

- The first task is to make the correct diagnosis.
- The second is to control the metabolic core of the disease with medication treatment.
- The third is to overcome phobic restrictions with behavior therapy.
- The fourth is to deal with psychosocial problems through psychotherapy.
- The fifth is to prevent relapses by educating the patient and ensuring long-term management.

Now that our overall strategy and the logic behind it has been outlined, let us consider these tasks in more detail in the next five chapters.

Much Madness is Divinist Sense—
To a discerning eye—

EMILY DICKINSON, No. 435

18. DIAGNOSIS

In this chapter we will review the series of diagnostic steps a doctor might take in trying to help any anxious patient. These steps are by no means the only way to diagnose the anxiety disease. Although they are not intended as a substitute for careful examination by a physician, anyone concerned that he or she has this condition may find it useful to work through the written exercises in this chapter.

Anyone who did not recognize one or more of the stages described in Chapters 4–11 is unlikely to have the disease. For anyone with spells such as those described in Chapter 4 or spontaneous panic attacks as described in Chapter 5, the first step is to obtain a thorough medical evaluation. The purpose of this is to rule out any medical illnesses that could cause these symptoms. All too often patients assume that a problem is psychosomatic or nervous in origin, only to find later that it is the initial symptom of a medical illness. This only delays their getting early and adequate treatment. Many

Figure 5. Decision tree for diagnosis of anxiety conditions

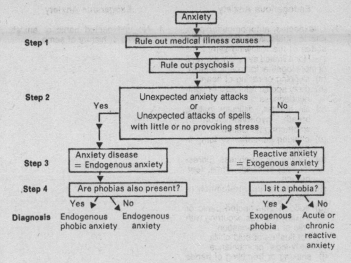

common as well as several exotic diseases, such as thyrotoxicosis, pheochromocytoma, and epilepsy; some infections, such as brucellosis; and neurological disorders, such as multiple sclerosis, can cause symptoms like those of the anxiety disease.

Every physician has been trained to check for these and other conditions that might produce similar symptoms. He may not mention to the patient all the conditions he is checking into, so as not to cause unnecessary alarm. But he is usually systematically ruling out these diseases as he checks the patient's general health.

After medical illness has been eliminated as a possible cause, the second step is to rule out psychiatric conditions that might present themselves in a similar way. The important psychiatric disorders to consider are the psychotic disorders. A person is said to have a psychosis when he or she has hallucinations and/or delusions. Hallucinations mean clearly seeing or hearing things that are not there; delusions are mistaken beliefs out of keeping with the person's background. For example, if someone described that he felt anxious because a voice had told him that he was Napoleon and that he was

————— Figure 6. Criteria for diagnosing anxiety —————

Endogenous Anxiety

1. Unexpected, autonomous, clonic, phasic (subjectively reported) episodes of the following symptoms (1–2 for a limited symptom attack, 3 or more together for a panic attack):
   (a) skipping or racing of heart
   (b) dizzy spells, faintness or light-headedness
   (c) air hunger, difficulty getting breath, hyperventilation or smothering sensation
   (d) choking sensation or lump in throat
   (e) tingling or numbness (pares-thesias) in hands, arms, feet, or face
   (f) nausea or upset stomach or vomiting
   (g) sudden unexpected panic or anxiety feelings occurring with little or no provocation
   (h) hot flushes or cold chills
   (i) "jelly-legs" or imbalance
   (j) shaking or trembling of hands or legs
   (k) feeling outside of or detached from part or all of your body or a floating feeling, feeling surroundings are strange, unreal, detached, unfamiliar or foggy
   (l) chest pain, pressure, or dis-comfort
   (m) fear of having a serious ill-ness or dying
   (n) feeling you will lose control, scream, "go insane"
   (o) spontaneous clonic alteration in sensory perception, e.g., in-creased clonic sensitivity to light, sound, touch, tempera-ture, taste, proprioception, or in muscle power
   (p) diarrhea attacks
   (q) sweating episodes unrelated to heat or exercise
2. Such symptom attacks have per-sistently recurred for at least one month. Within a three-month pe-riod, at least three discrete major attacks must occur for a diagnosis of major endogenous anxiety, or at least three discrete minor at-tacks for a diagnosis of minor en-dogenous anxiety

Exogenous Anxiety

1. No unexpected panic or anxiety attacks or history of same

2. Tension and symptoms of anxiety occur *only* in response to immediate, clear-cut, identifiable environmental stimuli. Onset of each attack not very sudden or unexpected but related to immediacy of triggering stimulus. In the case of conditioned changes in motor, sensory symptoms or spe-cial senses, the symptom may oc-cur alone without any overt anxiety

Endogenous Anxiety	Exogenous Anxiety
3. Phobic symptoms, particularly fear of a spontaneous panic attack (phobophobia), and fear of crowded places. Phobias start only after onset of first spontaneous attacks. Phobia may fluctuate in intensity over time	3. Phobia restricted to one specific focus. Monophobic rather than polyphobic. Phobia rarely fluctuates in intensity over time
4. Depression, neurasthenia (excessive tiredness and feeling everything is an effort), obsessive compulsive symptoms present to some degree in over two-thirds of cases	4. Depression, neurasthenia, obsessive compulsive symptoms, and other gross psychopathology absent
5. Anxiety profile of spontaneous attack as in Figure 3 (although anticipatory type may also occur)	5. Profile of anticipatory anxiety attack as in Figure 3
6. Spontaneous fluctuations on GSR (galvanic skin response)	6. No spontaneous fluctuations on GSR
7. Slow habituation rate on GSR	7. Normal or rapid habituation on GSR
8. Elevated resting pulse rate	8. Resting pulse within normal range
9. Brisk reflexes	9. Reflexes not hypertonic
10. Family history of anxiety attacks and phobic symptoms, especially among female relatives	10. Positive family history rare (insufficient data at this time)
11. Age of onset usually 12–40 years	11. May occur at any age.
12. 80% of cases occur in women	12. Approximately equal sex distribution (66% women)
13. More likely to have visited medical doctor and emergency ward several times for treatment of symptoms. Spontaneous anxiety must occur: in absence of medical illness that could cause such symptoms; in absence of life-threatening situations	13. Rarely seeks medical or emergency ward treatment
14. More likely to have seen several psychiatrists in treatment over many years	14. Multiple psychiatric consultations unlikely
15. More likely to have had a hospital admission and surgical treatment for symptoms	15. Multiple medical consultations unlikely
16. Response to MAO inhibitors and imipramine good	16. Response to drugs poor
17. Response of all symptoms to behavior therapy alone poor. Avoidance behavior alone may improve with exposure treatment, but not spontaneous attacks	17. Response to behavior therapy good
18. Autonomy of clonic phasic course (e.g., it has a life of its own that fluctuates over time, and it does not immediately improve when environmental circumstances seem favorable)	18. More clearly responsive to psychosocial stimulus
19. Anxiety attacks precipitated by sodium lactate and by marijuana	19. Anxiety attacks not precipitated by either sodium lactate or marijuana

going to be shipped into exile for being a cruel dictator, you might be skeptical. The hearing of the voice is a hallucination; the belief that he is Napoleon and being anxious about being sent into exile are delusions.

Common psychotic disorders include schizophrenia and manic depressive illness in its severe form. Acute intoxication or withdrawal from some drugs and sometimes alcohol can also lead to delusions or mistaken beliefs of being persecuted in bizarre ways that have no substance in reality. Withdrawal from alcohol can produce a psychotic disorder with hallucinations of touch and bizarre visual experiences known as delirium tremens. Psychiatrists are specially trained in how to diagnose and treat these conditions. If no obvious hallucinations or delusions are present, then it is unlikely that a psychosis is present, and the doctor moves to step 3.

At step 3 we ask whether the patient has ever had spells or spontaneous attacks that came with little or no provoking stress, such as those described in Stage 1 or Stage 2 of the disease. If the answer in either case is yes, it is quite possible that the anxiety disease is present. If on the other hand the patient's anxiety is not associated with either of these, but comes only in reaction to clear-cut stress or frightening situations, never surging suddenly with little or no provocation, then it is unlikely to be the anxiety disease. This can be referred to as exogenous anxiety because it appears only when events external to the patient trigger it and never appears otherwise. It is exclusively reactive. Figure 6 outlines diagnostic criteria for each of these two major subtypes of anxiety, which may be helpful in making the correct diagnosis at this step.

Step 4 is a refinement in the diagnosis. Are phobias present? is the question here. If they are, they add additional complications to the diagnosis since they will require some different approaches in treatment. This step is added to help in the selection of a proper approach. As will be seen later in the discussion on treatment, there is a different strategy for managing each of these types of anxiety diagnosis.

THE PATIENT-RATED ANXIETY SCALE

Scales can be useful in several areas of medical practice. Anxious patients often sense that their complaints are being carefully and thoroughly measured through these scales. For the doctor, scales offer a concise and accurate way of documenting major symptoms and judging their overall severity. Scales show at a glance which symptoms are most or least distressing; they also make it possible to measure a patient's improvement over time and judge his response to treatment.

The Patient-rated Anxiety Scale (Figure 7) has been divided into two parts. Part 1 measures the severity of the anxiety disease. This is filled out to reflect how the patient has felt over the past six months, especially when his condition was at its worst. Part 2 is used to measure the level of anxiety when the patient approaches his main phobia or finds himself facing it. How anxious or frightened did he get when the snake approached, or the beetle crawled up his arm? If many phobias are present—as is the case for most patients with the anxiety disease—Part 2 can be filled out several times, once for each main phobia. This provides a different score reflecting the level of severity of each major phobia.

Dividing the scale into two parts helps clarify the diagnosis. For example, if a patient scores low on Part 1 and high on Part 2, then it is possible that she does not have the anxiety disease; instead, she may have an exogenous anxiety or phobia. A high score on Part 1 and low on Part 2 indicates that a patient may have the anxiety disease, but still in an early stage and not yet complicated by many phobias. That will make treatment somewhat easier. High scores on both Part 1 and Part 2 probably indicate the presence of the anxiety disease, and at a more advanced stage of development complicated by phobias. We call this endogenous phobic anxiety, or the anxiety disease complicated by phobias, which is a more severe and advanced form. In a nutshell:

1. a low score on Part 1 + a high score on Part 2 = exogenous anxiety/phobia
2. a high score on Part 1 + a low score on Part 2 = endogenous anxiety
3. a high score on Parts 1 + 2 = endogenous phobic anxiety

────Figure 7. Patient-rated Anxiety Scale────

INSTRUCTIONS: Below is a list of problems and complaints that people sometimes have. Circle the number to the right that best describes how much that problem bothered or distressed you during the past six months. Mark only one number for each problem and do not skip any items.

0—Not at all **1**—A little bit **2**—Moderately **3**—Markedly **4**—Extremely

HOW MUCH DID YOU SUFFER FROM:

1. Lightheadedness, faintness or dizzy spells	0	1	2	3	4
2. Sensation of rubbery, weak or "jelly legs"	0	1	2	3	4
3. Feeling off-balance or unsteady as if about to fall	0	1	2	3	4
4. Difficulty in getting breath, smothering sensation, or overbreathing	0	1	2	3	4
5. Skipping or racing of the heart	0	1	2	3	4
6. Chest pain or pressure	0	1	2	3	4
7. Choking sensation or lump in throat	0	1	2	3	4
8. Tingling or numbness in parts of the body	0	1	2	3	4
9. Hot flashes or cold chills	0	1	2	3	4
10. Nausea or stomach problems	0	1	2	3	4
11. Episodes of diarrhea	0	1	2	3	4
12. Headaches or pains in neck or head	0	1	2	3	4
13. Feeling tired, weak, and exhausted easily	0	1	2	3	4
14. Spells of increased sensitivity to sound, light, or touch	0	1	2	3	4
15. Bouts of excessive sweating	0	1	2	3	4
16. Feeling that surroundings are strange, unreal, foggy, or detached	0	1	2	3	4
17. Feeling outside or detached from part or all of your body or a floating feeling	0	1	2	3	4
18. Worrying about your health too much	0	1	2	3	4
19. Feeling you are losing control or going insane	0	1	2	3	4
20. Having a fear that you are dying or that something terrible is about to happen	0	1	2	3	4
21. Shaking or trembling	0	1	2	3	4

22. Unexpected waves of depression occurring with little or no provocation   0 1 2 3 4

23. Emotions and moods going up and down a lot in response to changes around you   0 1 2 3 4

24. Being dependent on others   0 1 2 3 4

25. Having to repeat the same action in a ritual (e.g., checking, washing, counting repeatedly, when it's not really necessary)   0 1 2 3 4

26. Recurrent words or thoughts that persistently intrude on your mind and are hard to get rid of (e.g., unwanted aggressive, sexual, or poor impulse control thoughts)   0 1 2 3 4

27. Difficulty in falling asleep   0 1 2 3 4

28. Waking up in the middle of the night or restless sleep   0 1 2 3 4

29. Avoiding situations because they frighten you   0 1 2 3 4

30. Tension and inability to relax   0 1 2 3 4

31. Anxiety, nervousness, restlessness   0 1 2 3 4

32. Sudden anxiety attacks with three or more symptoms (listed above) that occur when you are in or about to go into a situation that from your experience is likely to bring on an attack   0 1 2 3 4

33. Sudden unexpected anxiety attacks with three or more symptoms occurring together that occur with little or no provocation (i.e., when you are *not* in a situation that is likely from your experience to bring on anxiety)   0 1 2 3 4

34. Sudden unexpected spells with only one or two symptoms that occur with little or no provocation (i.e., when you are *not* in a situation that is likely from your experience to bring on anxiety)   0 1 2 3 4

35. Anxiety episodes that build up as you anticipate doing something that is likely from your experience to bring on anxiety that is more intense than most people experience in such situations   0 1 2 3 4

115

─────── Figure 7. Patient-rated Anxiety Scale ───────

Part 2 ───

INSTRUCTIONS: Circle one of the numbers to the right of each question to describe how you feel in a phobic or stress situation

0—Not at all **1**—A little bit **2**—Moderately **3**—Markedly **4**—Extremely

1. Mouth drier than usual	0	1	2	3	4
2. Worried, preoccupied	0	1	2	3	4
3. Nervous, jittery, anxious, restless	0	1	2	3	4
4. Afraid, fearful	0	1	2	3	4
5. Tense, "uptight"	0	1	2	3	4
6. Shaky inside or out	0	1	2	3	4
7. Fluttery stomach	0	1	2	3	4
8. Warm all over	0	1	2	3	4
9. Sweaty palms	0	1	2	3	4
10. Rapid or heavy heartbeat	0	1	2	3	4
11. Tremor of hands or legs	0	1	2	3	4

Part 1

Score	6–30	mild endogenous anxiety
Score	31–50	moderate endogenous anxiety
Score	51–80	marked endogenous anxiety
Score	81–134	severe endogenous anxiety

Part 2

Score	4–11	mild exogenous anxiety or phobia
Score	12–22	moderate exogenous anxiety or phobia
Score	23–33	marked exogenous anxiety or phobia
Score	34–44	severe exogenous anxiety or phobia

Figure 8. Stage of disease checklist

		YES	NO
Stage 1	Spells (surges of symptoms)	___	___
Stage 2	Panic	___	___
Stage 3	Health worries	___	___
Stage 4	Limited phobias	___	___
Stage 5	Social phobias	___	___
Stage 6	Extensive phobias/agoraphobia	___	___
Stage 7	Depression	___	___

Knowing which of these three categories a patient belongs to helps the doctor select the best treatment approach later.

To calculate your score on the Patient-rated Anxiety Scale, add up all the numbers you marked. Calculate your total score for all of Part 1 and another score for all of Part 2. The following is a rough guide to the severity:

Figure 8 will help determine which stage of the disease a patient has entered. In the right-hand column of the chart, the patient checks yes or no as to whether he/she is in or has already passed through this stage. The more stages a patient has gone through, the more advanced, chronic, and severe the condition is likely to be.

THE GOOD NEWS

The good news is that no matter how severe or advanced the anxiety disease is, that should not make it less responsive to treatment. With proper handling, people in the advanced stages of the disease often do just as well as those with less chronic forms.

The second hopeful point is that much good research on this illness is now beginning. The biochemical aspects of the disorder are undergoing careful study. It is likely that in the near future blood, urine, and other lab tests will be developed that will help in diagnosis. Much of the research now going on is setting the groundwork for this—it is only a matter of time. When such tests are available, the whole view of the condition will change. It will be taken seriously, not considered as merely "neurotic" or "nervous," and will also be diagnosed earlier and more accurately. This in turn will lead to more effective treatment and more precise assessment of improvement.

Medicines are nothing in themselves,
if not properly used,
but the very hands of the gods,
if employed with reason and prudence.

HEROPHILUS, 300 B.C.

19. *TARGET 1: BIOLOGICAL*

Many patients worry about using drugs to correct their anxiety disease, fearing that they will be merely tranquilized into a passive state. Fortunately, in the past several years, doctors have become much more sophisticated and precise in their choice and use of psychiatric medications. There is now a wide range of drugs with extremely specific effects that do not leave patients in a "drugged" state.

DRUG CHOICE

The five families of medication that appear to be effective in controlling the anxiety disease are listed below in boldface. The generic names of drugs within each family are listed below the family names, with the trade names under which these drugs are sold in parentheses beside them.

Monoamine oxidase inhibitors (MAO inhibitors) This family includes three drugs:
    phenelzine (Nardil)
    isocarboxazid (Marplan)
    tranylcypromine (Parnate)
Tricyclic antidepressants There are many members of this class. The most widely used and studied are:
    imipramine (Tofranil)
    desipramine (Norpramin)
    amitriptyline (Elavil)
    maprotiline (Ludiomil)
Triazolopyridine
    trazodone (Desyrel)
Tetracyclic antidepressant
    Mianserin (Tolvon)
Benzodiazepine
    alprazolam (Xanax)
    clonazepam (klonopin)
    diazepam
5HT-Reuptake Inhibitors
    Fluoxetine (Prozac)

Some individuals respond better to one of these drugs than to the others for reasons that are still unclear. For the purposes of simplicity, some generalizations may be helpful. It appears that the MAO inhibitors, particularly phenelzine, are the single most effective drugs overall for the anxiety disease. The disadvantage of the MAO inhibitor family is that they are somewhat more difficult to prescribe and regulate than the other families. They are also associated with increases in blood pressure in people who eat foods that contain a substance called tyramine (e.g., cheese). If a few foods, drinks, and medications are avoided, there is no reason why this should occur, and most patients adjust easily to these dietary restrictions. However, because many physicians are fearful that their patients will not follow their directions, they are very reluctant to prescribe this type of medication. It is also more demanding and difficult to regulate correctly, and requires greater skill on the part of the physician. In general, drugs in the MAO inhibitor family should only be given to patients who are careful and conscientious in following direc-

experienced in their use. Overall they have the biggest disadvantage.

The tricyclic antidepressants are widely used in the treatment of severe depression. Of the four listed, desipramine has the fewest side effects and causes least drowsiness, while amitriptyline has the most side effects and causes most drowsiness. Imipramine, the mother of all the tricyclic antidepressants, is a good compromise and has been studied intensely. Other members of the tricyclic family of medicines also appear to be effective, although they have been less well studied in this disorder. Although these drugs are usually very effective when correctly used, they do have significant side effects that cause many patients disruption during the first few weeks. They have no food and drug restrictions like MAO inhibitors; but they can be more irritating to the heart, and in rare cases can trigger seizures.

Trazodone and maprotiline are two new drugs recently introduced. They have not been studied for as long or as intensely as the MAO inhibitors or the tricyclics; also the evidence for their effectiveness in controlling the anxiety disease, though very promising, is still preliminary. Trazodone is somewhat less disruptive than the others mentioned above, but can cause drowsiness at first. It is also sometimes effective in cases that fail to respond to any of the other families of drugs.

In general, all four of the medications just described have two significant disadvantages: they are somewhat disruptive and unpleasant to take during the first few weeks; and they need a minimum of three to four weeks before providing significant sustained control over the spontaneous attacks. It is not realistic for most patients to expect an effect sooner.

Although beta-blocking drugs such as propranolol are frequently used for anxiety symptoms, they are usually only partially effective at best in the treatment of the anxiety disease. They are helpful in blocking some of the symptoms of the condition, particularly racing of the heart and hand tremor. Their most useful role is in the treatment of performance anxiety in someone who does not suffer from the anxiety disease.

Alprazolam is another new medication, which has several important advantages over the others. First, it seems to work immediately, within the first few days or once a satisfactory dose is reached. It has fewer side effects and is much less disruptive to take than the others. But like all medications, it too has drawbacks. Most patients find it causes some sleepiness or drowsiness, particularly when they are passive or relaxing. For some people it is not as effective an antidepressant as the MAO inhibitors and tricyclics; and it has to be taken on a more frequent schedule to keep the disorder under solid control.

Because these drugs appear effective, the choice is usually made on the basis of which side effects seem most comfortable to live with and how much power is needed to control the disease. Frequently in choosing a drug with fewer side effects, some power is lost. The ultimate solution must be a trade-off, with no easy winners.

DRUG SEQUENCE

Which drug is the best to start with? Again, this is not an easy choice. Individual circumstances may dictate the use of one over another. As new research evolves and new medications emerge, these guidelines are always changing. At this time we might generalize by saying that following the course outlined in Figure 9 is my own present preference. In this strategy, the goal is to keep on until complete recovery is reached. For example, let us consider that a patient is diagnosed as having pure endogenous anxiety, using the scale in Figure 5 (p. 109), and also satisfies all the items for this diagnosis listed in Figure 6 (p. 110). He may be started on alprazolam. Unlike other benzodiazepines such as Valium and Librium, this triazolo compound appears to possess anti-spontaneous panic attack effects. These may be due in part to the extra triazolo ring on its chemical structure, which distinguishes it from the conventional tranquilizers. Alprazolam is also the most rapidly effective of the anti-panic drugs, and the least disruptive and least toxic to the patient. For all these reasons, it appears to be the safest to use, and it is the easiest for the physician to prescribe, regulate, and monitor.

The major reason for choosing alprazolam is, then, first its relatively superior safety and speed of action. It is not

Figure 9. Management strategy for endogenous anxiety

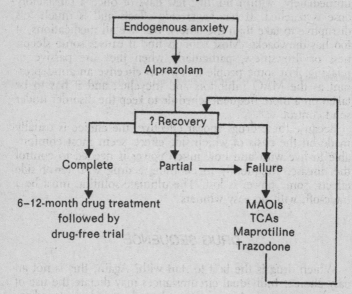

necessarily more powerful than the others and is not without disadvantages. For example, since it is an anti-seizure drug, it cannot be abruptly stopped lest it lead to disruptive withdrawal. This can be minimized by a slow tapering off of the dose. After two or three weeks of treatment an adequate dose on the completeness of recovery is evaluated. If panic attacks have ceased, then the patient may be kept on the medication for several months, after which the drug may be slowly tapered off over a few weeks. At this point some patients may be able to manage free of symptoms without medication. Others will not.

If recovery is only partial after an adequate trial of alprazolam, then it should be regarded as a treatment failure and the dose slowly lowered. The physician next chooses either an MAO inhibitor, a tricyclic, a triazolopyridine, or a tetracyclic. The choice is best predicated on an individual basis for each patient and physician: the relative benefits and side effects of each drug must be considered. Figure 10 is provided as an approximate guide to help in making that choice.

The numbers cited in Figure 10 reflect the strength or likelihood of a specific effect from each drug on a ten-point scale when compared to other drugs. The higher the score given, the greater the chance of that effect occurring when it is compared with the others. If a specific side effect causes problems, then switching to another effective drug with less of that particular side effect may be indicated. If more of a certain treatment benefit is required, then switching to another drug with more of that effect might be helpful.

In general, the MAO inhibitor phenelzine remains the most effective drug at this time. It is, however, offset by some troublesome side effects and the necessity of a low tyramine diet.

As a rule, these drugs are rarely significantly effective in less than three weeks. If a patient has been at an adequate dose for six to eight weeks without benefit, the drug should be changed to the next in the series of families outlined. After six to eight weeks it too is evaluated to see how well it has provided recovery. The strategy outlined in Figure 9 (p. 122) calls for following the lines until recovery is complete.

DOSE ADJUSTMENT

To make another generalization about drug treatment, it is fair to say that correct adjustment of the dose of any of these effective drugs is more critical to a good result than choice of which drug to use. Doctors who specialize in this disorder are frequently referred patients who have been on several of the medications listed, but who still have symptoms. The specialist then focuses his or her attention on fine-tuning the dose— usually increasing and manipulating it to achieve the improvement that should have come sooner. Often small increases in dose are all that are needed.

Another generalization is that the dose at which the patient gets the optimal improvement is the dose at which he or she experiences some of the typical side effects of the medication. If patients are not experiencing any of these side effects, they may not yet be on the best dose to achieve full benefit. The skill lies in fine-tuning the dose to squeeze out maximum benefit without incurring too many side effects.

Figure 10. Merits and disadvantages of several anti-panic drugs

Numbers reflect the strength or likelihood of the drug's effects, on a ten-point scale, as compared with the others. If a specific side effect causes problems, use of an effective agent that is less likely to produce the effect may be indicated. If greater therapeutic effect is desired in a particular area, use of a drug that is more likely to have the effect may be helpful. Weights are based on the author's clinical experience and are offered as clinical guides rather than statements of scientific fact.

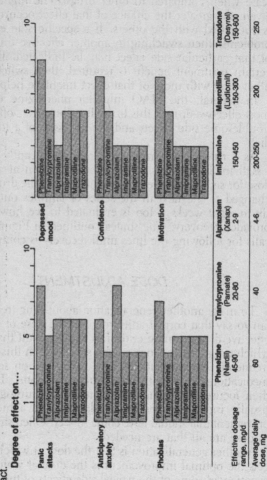

Degree of effect on...

	Phenelzine (Nardil) 45-90	Tranylcypromine (Parnate) 20-80	Alprazolam (Xanax) 2-9	Imipramine 150-450	Maprotiline (Ludiomil) 150-300	Trazodone (Desyrel) 150-600
Effective dosage range, mg/d						
Average daily dose, mg	60	40	4-6	200-250	200	250

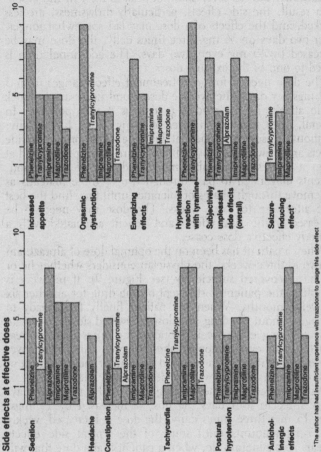

Side effects at effective doses

Increased appetite
- Phenelzine
- Tranylcypromine
- Imipramine
- Maprotiline
- Trazodone

Orgasmic dysfunction
- Phenelzine
- Tranylcypromine
- Imipramine
- Maprotiline
- Trazodone

Energizing effects
- Phenelzine
- Tranylcypromine
- Imipramine
- Maprotiline
- Trazodone

Hypertensive reaction with tyramine
- Phenelzine
- Tranylcypromine

Subjectively unpleasant side effects (overall)
- Phenelzine
- Tranylcypromine
- Alprazolam
- Imipramine
- Maprotiline
- Trazodone

Seizure-inducing effect*
- Tranylcypromine
- Imipramine
- Maprotiline

Sedation
- Phenelzine
- Tranylcypromine
- Alprazolam
- Imipramine
- Maprotiline
- Trazodone

Headache
- Alprazolam

Constipation
- Phenelzine
- Tranylcypromine
- Alprazolam
- Imipramine
- Maprotiline
- Trazodone

Tachycardia
- Phenelzine
- Tranylcypromine
- Imipramine
- Maprotiline
- Trazodone

Postural hypotension
- Phenelzine
- Tranylcypromine
- Imipramine
- Maprotiline
- Trazodone

Anticholinergic effects
- Phenelzine
- Tranylcypromine
- Imipramine
- Maprotiline
- Trazodone

*The author has had insufficient experience with trazodone to gauge this side effect

Sheehan, David V., "Current Views on the Treatment of Panic and Phobic Disorders," (*Drug Therapy,* September 1982).

With alprazolam, the usual starting dose is ½ milligram (mg) three times daily. A dose is taken at the end of each meal. If the doses are taken after food, the drug is absorbed more slowly and its level does not peak as high in the blood. As a result, the side effects, particularly drowsiness, are less marked, and the effects of a dose may last somewhat longer. After two days on ½ mg three times daily, the dose may be increased by ½ mg every two days. The additional dose is added to one of the existing doses.

The dose needed for good treatment effects ranges from 3 to 9 mgs per day. The average dose found necessary to block panic attacks in the studies to date is 6 mgs per day. In general, after reaching a level of 2 mgs three times daily, additional doses are added at bedtime. The principal side effects are drowsiness, unsteadiness, slurring of speech, and at times a depressed, irritable mood and lack of motivation. Patients may need to pass through two or three plateaus as they move through phases of tolerance until they find the best dose after one to three weeks. The dose may need to be increased if the side effects and benefit associated with a formerly effective dose cease.

When a patient has been on the optimal dose of alprazolam for two to three weeks, the physician considers whether he or she has recovered sufficiently (see Figure 9). If recovery is complete, the patient is still kept on the drug for another six to twelve months. When the patient finally feels ready to manage without the drug, the dose is lowered slowly, at a rate of ½ to 1 mg every week. None of the drugs used to treat anxiety should ever be stopped abruptly, even if it is ineffective. To do so might trigger a rebound flare-up of the condition or possibly serious withdrawal effects or even a seizure.

With phenelzine, the starting dose is 15 mgs per day. Every three to four days the dose is increased by 15 mgs. After 15 mgs three times daily, the dose is increased weekly by 15-mg amounts until some of the typical side effects appear. As a general rule, when a patient is at a dose that will provide a good result, the standing blood pressure (as compared to the blood pressure seated at rest) drops a little. For this reason, checking the blood pressure sitting and standing and keeping an accurate record of it regularly is advisable. (For more details on the use and side effects of MAO inhibitors in psychiatric treatment, as well as in-depth guidelines on the use and side effects of some other drugs such as the tricyclics, see Further Reading at the back of the book.)

With all these drugs, the presence of some typical side effects is usually necessary to ensure that the patient has achieved an adequate dose. Clinical skill and careful adjustment are essential to strike a comfortable balance between benefits and side effects. It is probably fair to say that at this stage historically in the introduction of these drugs, the doses most frequently prescribed are often less than adequate to achieve the best results. Patience and persistence are needed by both patient and physician to reach the goal of the best possible long-term dose.

EDUCATING THE PATIENT

The medicines that are effective for this disorder can neither be prescribed nor consumed casually. Any physician can of course prescribe them. However, it is reassuring to know that there are medical specialists called psychopharmacologists who devote most of their time to treating patients with these medications, following recent advances in the area, and researching them thoroughly. Psychopharmacologists specialize in drugs that influence the mind or central nervous system; they are almost all physicians who first specialize in psychiatry and later do further work in drug treatment. For patients seeking the expert opinion of these specialists, one referral sequence would be as follows: first locate the nearest medical school, then locate the department of psychiatry within that medical school. (Most medical schools in the United States have departments of psychiatry located in several nearby university-affiliated teaching hospitals.) Then consult the staff of the psychopharmacology units within those hospitals. They may be able to help themselves, but if they are located too far away, they will usually make a referral to a colleague competent in psychopharmacology closer to the patient's home.

Many psychiatrists are now well trained in psychopharmacology and can be very helpful. Psychologists do not have an M.D. degree or medical training like psychiatrists, so by law they are not permitted to prescribe medications. However, they are frequently well trained in behavior therapy. As we will see in the next chapter, this type of treatment is also often helpful, especially after the medication has controlled the spontaneous attacks. Specialists in behavior therapy can frequently provide further dimension to the improvement. Their methods are especially helpful in overcoming phobias.

Many psychologists now work with psychiatrists as a team. With this arrangement, the effective medications can be prescribed and monitored by the psychiatrist. The psychologist then helps provide further treatment for other targets if needed. Such a team is likely to include specialists who are sensitive and knowledgeable about each other's areas of expertise.

Prescribing medications for the anxiety disease is not unlike prescribing insulin for a diabetic. Diabetics have to learn a good deal and work closely with the medical team to get the best possible control over their diabetes. The time of day the insulin is taken, the dose at each of these times, whether it is taken with or without food, all are important considerations. In addition, attention must be paid to levels of exercise and intake of adequate fluids. With most chronic illnesses, this careful monitoring of medication and working with an informed patient can make the difference between a mediocre and a good result. Treating the anxiety disease is very similar.

Time spent with the physician in the early stages of treatment is well rewarded. He will outline and discuss the treatment strategy and the choice of medication. Many physicians provide written guidelines as to how to start and build up the medication dose, as well as printed information on how to manage various side effects and problems that commonly arise. Although it can be alarming at first to realize that side effects may occur, it is easy to learn which of these are good guides to the correct dose, which are not dangerous, and which are troublesome.

Time spent by the doctor and patient on these matters not only relieves worry and anxiety in the long run but renders them allies in treatment. This improves the chances that the patient will follow the doctor's directions and work with him rather than against him in seeking the best possible result, and that the doctor will understand the patient better. Some patients find it helpful to take notes or even bring a tape recorder to their treatment sessions. This captures the details of instructions in a precise yet time-saving fashion.

Learning more about the condition and its treatment is usually helpful in the long run. Sometimes patients are frightened by some of what they read; as they learn more, they come to understand that the benefits of these treatments significantly outweigh the disadvantages. They realize that their physicians are cautious in protecting them against harm. In turn, their health interests with medications are further capably protected by the Food and Drug Administration, which carefully scrutinizes all drugs and how they are prescribed, and constantly reviews information on side effects to protect the public from any major hazards.

In Chapter 17, The Four Targets of Treatment, we saw how Adam sought out more detailed information on the anxiety disease and its treatment. Many patients do not realize how easy it is to seek the best quality information. Working with a trained librarian often produces much information that is helpful to a patient or the family; they should not be discouraged from reading the journals and textbooks available to doctors and specialists. People are often surprised by how much of this material they can follow. We are in an information era—one might even say an information revolution—and there is no reason why the average lay person cannot participate. At times, reading such textbooks, patients are disappointed at the diversity of opinion, even the amount of disagreement on any topic. They soon learn that this is part of the method of science. There is a constant struggle between opposing viewpoints—in the long run, the best of the new ideas survive and a new consensus of opinion emerges. But the process is always evolving, improving, always seeking greater accuracy and truth.

Educating and informing the patient will become increasingly important in the years to come. It has been said that a little knowledge is a dangerous thing for patients in medicine. The best treatment for this problem is to prescribe more and better information, rather than discouraging access to it in the first place.

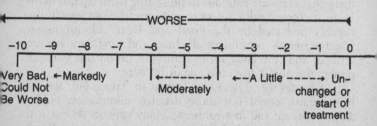

Figure 11. Patients' and Physicians' Global Improvement Scale

INSTRUCTIONS: Circle a number that best describes your situation now.
Since starting this treatment my overall progress is:

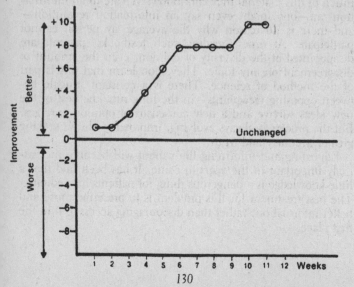

Figure 12. Changes in Global Improvement Score with treatment

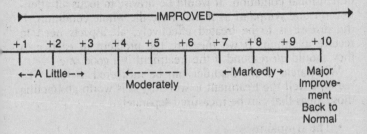

←————————————IMPROVED————————————→

+1   +2   +3   +4   +5   +6   +7   +8   +9   +10

←–A Little–→   ←– – – – – –→   ←Markedly→   Major
                    Moderately   Improve-
                                                       ment
                                                       Back to
                                                       Normal

MONITORING RESPONSE
AND COMPLICATIONS

"How are you doing?" and "Any problems?" are routine questions a physician asks—deceptively simple, easily passed off and ignored. Yet these questions tap a vast reservoir. The better the system used to probe this reservoir, the more valuable and useful is the yield of information; and the better the yield, the more likely it will lead to a good treatment. We need a clear-cut yardstick, then, by which to measure the patient's condition and to keep track of side effects and complications.

MONITORING OVERALL IMPROVEMENT

The simplest way of measuring improvement is to use a Global Improvement Scale like the one in Figure 11. Each week (or at regular intervals) this is scored. After a few weeks the number can easily be plotted out on a graph as shown in Figure 12.

At a glance, it is easy to see how much has been accomplished but also, just as important, the distance that still needs to be traveled. The patient and doctor focus their attention on this, identifying what it is precisely that needs to be done and how best to do it.

As we saw in earlier chapters, this is not a simple disease with one or two identifying symptoms; rather, it is a multidimensional condition. It would be unwise to focus all attention on one symptom as if that were the whole condition. If the disease is to be treated effectively, all aspects need to receive attention. If we measure the problem in each area they should *all* respond if the treatment is a good one.

What areas of the disorder can be measured usefully? To see how well the treatment is working, it is worth abstracting those areas that can be measured separately.

- The symptoms
- The attacks themselves
- The phobias
- The disability that results
- The side effects of drug treatment.

Monitoring Symptoms

Symptoms can be measured using the Patient-rated Anxiety Scale (Figure 7, p. 116). Part 1 of this scale will score the spells of symptoms occurring regularly; Part 2 can give a different score for each of the main phobias, depending on the anxiety experienced in each one. Your goal is to keep lowering the scores until all are down to zero or close to it. This provides you with a measure of how well you are doing.

Monitoring Attacks

Panic and anxiety attacks can be measured using the attack profile shown in Figure 13. Figure 18 (p. 142) can be used as a guide to distinguish the different attacks from each other. In Part A you consider the attacks that come with little or no provocation. Of these, attacks that had three or more symptoms occurring together in the same episode are recorded as

Figure 13. Panic and Anxiety Attack Scale

	Number in past week	Number in past month	Average length (min-utes)	Average intensity (0–10)
Part A: Panic Attacks				
Situational Panic Attacks: sudden anxiety attacks with 3 or more symptoms that occurred when in or just about to go into a situation likely from experience to bring on an attack.	_____	_____	_____	_____
Unexpected Panic Attacks: sudden unexpected anxiety attacks with 3 or more symptoms that occurred with little or no provocation (i.e. when NOT in a situation likely to bring on an attack.)	_____	_____	_____	_____
Part B: Limited Symptom Attacks				
Situational limited symptom attacks: sudden attacks limited to 1 or 2 symptoms that occurred when in or just about to enter a situation likely from experience to bring on an attack.	_____	_____	_____	_____
Unexpected limited symptom attacks: sudden attacks limited to 1 or 2 symptoms that occurred with little or no provocation (i.e. when NOT in or just about to enter a situation likely from experience to bring on an attack.)	_____	_____	_____	_____
Part C: Anticipatory Anxiety Episodes				
anxiety that occurs in anticipation of facing a phobic situation or of having a panic attack.	_____	_____	% of waking time spent anxiously anticipating % _____	_____

unexpected panic attacks. Attacks that only strike one or two parts of the body are counted as minor spontaneous attacks.

Part B is for recording anxiety attacks that are associated with clear-cut situations you fear and avoid. Under "anticipatory anxiety episodes" you count the number of times you had a buildup of anxiety as you anticipated going into situations that you fear and avoid. Sudden surges of panic that occur while you are in a phobic situation are recorded as situational panic attacks. For example, if you fear crowded supermarkets, you may get a buildup of anxiety as you approach it and wonder, "What if I get a panic attack in there?" This is an anticipatory anxiety episode. If you then go into the supermarket and several minutes later get a sudden surge of panic, that is a situational panic attack. Situational panic attacks are often superimposed on anticipatory anxiety.

With each of these four types of attacks you may wish to record how long the average one lasts, even if it varies, and how intense the average one is, even if it varies. The intensity is measured up to 10, where 10 is the maximum possible. A zero on this scale is complete relaxation. As you improve with treatment, the scores on all of these will get lower and lower. If you like, you can plot these out on a graph also.

Monitoring Phobias

Phobias can be measured using the Phobia Scale shown in Figure 14. This scale includes a spectrum of phobias frequently found in patients with the anxiety disease. Item 1 asks you to pick the main phobia (situation or thing you avoid) that you want treated. Every week you score this item, you keep the same phobias in this space. In the first column you choose a score from 0 to 10, using the scale at the top as a guide, and enter it based on how anxious being in that situation makes you. Then in the next columns you make a check mark in the box that tells how much you avoid that situation. At the bottom of the page is an overall scale—to give a quick overview on how bad all your phobias taken together are. Over time, as you improve, all these scores should get lower. When they remain high in any area, you and your doctor will focus efforts on that area of treatment.

Monitoring Disability

The symptoms of the anxiety disease disable people to varying degrees in different areas of their life. Obviously, this too must be overcome. The Disability Scale shown in Figure 15 measures this in a simple, direct way.

At the beginning of treatment, the scores on this scale are usually high; within two to three months, they should be very low. In general, the longer patients have been on an effective treatment, the lower their scores. The biggest improvement occurs on all the scales in the first four to six weeks. However, with each passing month there should be a further reduction in all scores. Above all it is important not to settle for a partial or second-rate improvement. Very good results are frequently possible; often all that is necessary is a small increase in the medication. Here persistence and patience are well repaid.

Monitoring Side Effects

A checklist for measuring some side effects typically found with the various effective drugs for this condition is shown in Figure 16. This can be scored at the end of each day or each week, or before each visit to the doctor, to cover all the side effects that occurred since the last visit. It will save the physician much time and trouble, allowing him to focus on the items he is most interested in. The overall score on this checklist also will change over time. Usually the scores are highest in the first few weeks of treatment; after that, they taper off. Once again this provides a way of keeping track. With the tricyclics and MAO inhibitors some patients experience side effects during the first several weeks of treatment that are very unpleasant subjectively. This often frightens patients who are already very anxious and prompts many of them to prematurely stop taking their medicines, resulting in unnecessary treatment failures. Usually these unpleasant side effects will lessen significantly after about a month, so patience and perseverance at this point is well repaid. They rarely become long-term problems, and the great majority of them are not serious, however unpleasant and frightening they

────── Figure 14. Phobia Scale ──────

To fill out the phobia scale below, circle a number between 0 and 10 in the top row of each section to show how much you fear a situation, and a number between 0 and 4 in the bottom row to show how much you avoid that situation. Use the scales below as a guide.

How much do you *fear* the situations named below?

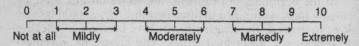

How much do you *avoid* the situations named below:

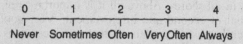

1. Main phobias you want treated

   Phobia 1 Specify: Fear   0 1 2 3 4 5 6 7 8 9 10
                   Avoidance 0 1 2 3 4

   Phobia 2 Specify: Fear   0 1 2 3 4 5 6 7 8 9 10
                   Avoidance 0 1 2 3 4

   Phobia 3 Specify: Fear   0 1 2 3 4 5 6 7 8 9 10
                   Avoidance 0 1 2 3 4

   Phobia 4 Specify: Fear   0 1 2 3 4 5 6 7 8 9 10
                   Avoidance 0 1 2 3 4

2. Going far from home alone   Fear   0 1 2 3 4 5 6 7 8 9 10

3. Sudden unexpected attacks of panic/anxiety that occur with little or no cause   Fear   0 1 2 3 4 5 6 7 8 9 10
       Avoidance 0 1 2 3 4

4. Traveling on buses, subways, trains, or in cars   Fear   0 1 2 3 4 5 6 7 8 9 10
       Avoidance 0 1 2 3 4

5. Crowded places (e.g., shopping, sports events, theaters)   Fear   0 1 2 3 4 5 6 7 8 9 10
       Avoidance 0 1 2 3 4

6.	Large open spaces	Fear	0 1 2 3 4 5 6 7 8 9 10
		Avoidance	0 1 2 3 4
7.	Feeling trapped or caught in closed spaces	Fear	0 1 2 3 4 5 6 7 8 9 10
		Avoidance	0 1 2 3 4
8.	Being left alone	Fear	0 1 2 3 4 5 6 7 8 9 10
		Avoidance	0 1 2 3 4
9.	The thought of physical injury or illness	Fear	0 1 2 3 4 5 6 7 8 9 10
		Avoidance	0 1 2 3 4
10.	Hearing or reading about health topics or disease	Fear	0 1 2 3 4 5 6 7 8 9 10
		Avoidance	0 1 2 3 4
11.	Eating, drinking, or writing in public	Fear	0 1 2 3 4 5 6 7 8 9 10
		Avoidance	0 1 2 3 4
12.	Being watched or being the focus of attention	Fear	0 1 2 3 4 5 6 7 8 9 10
		Avoidance	0 1 2 3 4
13.	Being with others because you are very self-conscious	Fear	0 1 2 3 4 5 6 7 8 9 10
		Avoidance	0 1 2 3 4
14.	Situations other than those listed above that you fear and avoid:	Fear	0 1 2 3 4 5 6 7 8 9 10
		Avoidance	0 1 2 3 4
15.	Specify farthest distance you can go alone:	Yards _____
		Miles _____

Rate the present state of your phobias overall on the scale below. Circle the number you select.

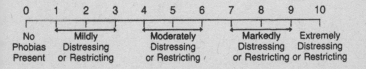

| 0 | 1 | 2 | 3 | 4 | 5 | 6 | 7 | 8 | 9 | 10 |

| No Phobias Present | Mildly Distressing or Restricting | Moderately Distressing or Restricting | Markedly Distressing or Restricting | Extremely Distressing or Restricting |

This scale was adapted from the work of I. M. Marks and A. Mathews and modified for use in the United States by the author. Those interested in the original work can consult the book *Living with Fear* (see Further Reading).

137

Figure 15. Disability Scale

INSTRUCTIONS: Circle a number that best describes your situation now.

WORK

The symptoms have disrupted your work

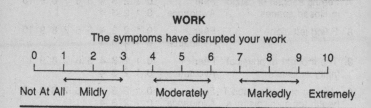

0   1   2   3   4   5   6   7   8   9   10

Not At All   Mildly   Moderately   Markedly   Extremely

SOCIAL LIFE/LEISURE ACTIVITIES

The symptoms have disrupted your social life

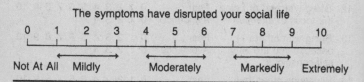

0   1   2   3   4   5   6   7   8   9   10

Not At All   Mildly   Moderately   Markedly   Extremely

FAMILY LIFE/HOME RESPONSIBILITIES

The symptoms have disrupted your family life/home responsibilities

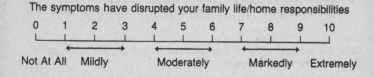

0   1   2   3   4   5   6   7   8   9   10

Not At All   Mildly   Moderately   Markedly   Extremely

are in the short term. If patients are prepared to expect a short period of disruptive side effects and are encouraged to persist through it, working closely with their doctor to make the necessary dose adjustments rather than giving up, then the chances are high that they will see it through successfully.

If maintaining all the charts in this chapter proves too cumbersome, using a simple diary between visits like that shown in Figure 17 to record attacks, side effects, and dosage each day is often helpful. The type of attack occurring each day should be recorded, along with the total dose, how it was taken, and any significant side effects on the day they occurred.

Above all, it is helpful to doctors when patients keep accurate notes and bring copies to their visits. My patients have taught me that this is useful to them too, and they have shown me the systems they found most efficient. Their notes help them remember any important questions they want to ask. Too often anxious people become forgetful in their doctor's presence, yet they often have much to report and much to ask him. The scales suggested above provide both patient and doctor with a clear-cut system.

Many patients have given me organized (even typed) information like this neatly laid out with headings at each visit, and it has been pure pleasure to treat them. Not only has it made my work easy, but it has provided the necessary information to get the best possible results for them. It has given me greater confidence in them as reliable, responsible people. It has also taught me that as physicians we have much to learn from our patients. Given the opportunity, they are only too eager to be our helpful allies in controlling and coping with their disease.

Figure 16. Side-effects checklist for anti-panic, anti-anxiety, and anti-phobic medications

INSTRUCTIONS: Please indicate whether you experienced any of the following symptoms during the past week. Circle the number that best describes how much that problem bothered or distressed you.

0—Not at all **1**—A little bit **2**—Moderately **3**—Markedly **4**—Extremely

1. Headaches	0	1	2	3	4
2. Difficulty falling asleep	0	1	2	3	4
3. Waking up a lot during the night	0	1	2	3	4
4. Nightmares	0	1	2	3	4
5. Agitation/restlessness	0	1	2	3	4
6. Fine tremor	0	1	2	3	4
7. Seizures	0	1	2	3	4
8. Unsteadiness/poor coordination	0	1	2	3	4
9. Fatigue/weakness	0	1	2	3	4
10. Confusion	0	1	2	3	4
11. Irritability	0	1	2	3	4
12. Sadness/depression	0	1	2	3	4
13. Decrease in appetite	0	1	2	3	4
14. Weight loss	0	1	2	3	4
15. Increased appetite	0	1	2	3	4
16. Weight gain	0	1	2	3	4
17. Fluid retention in ankles or fingers	0	1	2	3	4
18. Sweating	0	1	2	3	4
19. Nausea/vomiting	0	1	2	3	4
20. Constipation	0	1	2	3	4
21. Faintness/dizziness	0	1	2	3	4
22. Difficulty emptying bladder	0	1	2	3	4
23. Blurred vision	0	1	2	3	4
24. Palpitations (skipping or racing of heart)	0	1	2	3	4
25. Dry mouth	0	1	2	3	4
26. Hot flashes/cold chills	0	1	2	3	4
27. Diarrhea	0	1	2	3	4
28. Skin rashes	0	1	2	3	4
29. Jaundice	0	1	2	3	4
30. Sedation/sleepiness	0	1	2	3	4
31. Too much energy	0	1	2	3	4
32. Muscle twitching	0	1	2	3	4
33. Forgetting things	0	1	2	3	4
34. Being too aggressive/assertive	0	1	2	3	4
35. Talking too much	0	1	2	3	4
36. Hearing or seeing things you know weren't there	0	1	2	3	4
37. Distortions in the shape of things	0	1	2	3	4
38. Electric shock sensations	0	1	2	3	4
39. Inability to have erections (in males)	0	1	2	3	4
40. Inability to ejaculate/reach orgasm	0	1	2	3	4
41. Other (specify)	0	1	2	3	4
42. Other (specify)	0	1	2	3	4
43. Other (specify)	0	1	2	3	4

Figure 17. Panic attack diary

PANIC ATTACK (3 or more symptoms)

1. Situational [TYPE 1]
   Sudden anxiety attack with three or more symptoms that occurs when you are in or about to go into a situation likely from your experience to bring on an attack.

2. Unexpected [TYPE 2]
   Sudden unexpected anxiety attack with three or more symptoms that occurs with little or no provocation, i.e. when NOT in a situation likely to bring on an attack.

LIMITED SYMPTOM ATTACK (1 or 2 symptoms)

3. Situational [TYPE 3]
   Sudden attack limited to 1 or 2 symptoms when you are in or about to enter a situation likely from experience to bring on an attack.

4. Unexpected [TYPE 4]
   Sudden attack limited to 1 or 2 symptoms that occurs with little or no provocation, i.e. when NOT in a situation likely from experience to bring on an attack.

ANTICIPATORY ANXIETY

5. [TYPE 5]
   Anxious worrying about having a panic attack or anxious worrying about going in to a situation likely in your experience to bring on anxiety.

INSTRUCTIONS: When you get a Type 1, 2, 3, 4 or 5 attack write that number into that day's box. Enter one of these numbers each time you have an attack.

Mon.	Tues.	Wed.	Thurs.	Fri.	Sat.	Sun.
Mon.	Tues.	Wed.	Thurs.	Fri.	Sat.	Sun.
Mon.	Tues.	Wed.	Thurs.	Fri.	Sat.	Sun.

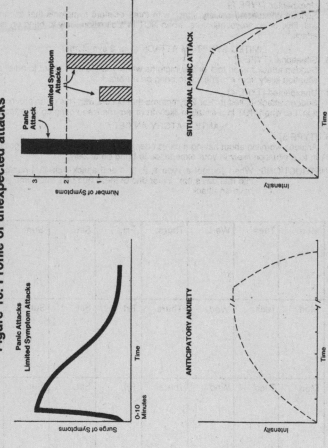

Figure 18. Profile of unexpected attacks

And what they dare to dream of, dare to do.

JAMES RUSSELL LOWELL, *Ode Recited at the
Harvard Commemoration* [1865]

20. *TARGET 2: PHOBIAS*

Frequently, medication is all that is needed to control the
anxiety disease. When the spontaneous attacks stop, patients
may feel confident enough to go out again into situations
they had been avoiding. They quickly become comfortable in
these situations with a little practice. This is more likely to be
the case when the disease has only recently started or is not
very severe.

The medications in general work best against the metabolic
core of the disease: they block the unexpected attacks. Their
effect on the phobias is less obvious and less immediate.
Ultimately the patient has to go back into the phobic situation
a few times to feel comfortable there. It is not unusual for
some phobias to be so severe and intense that the patient,
although much improved in other ways, still resists going
back into the situation. When a phobia is this deeply ingrained, the patient may need behavior therapy to help him
or her overcome it.

Behavior therapy embraces several techniques of treatment. These include such methods as systematic desensitization, flooding, relaxation training, cognitive restructuring, exposure in vivo, and response prevention. But although all these methods may sound different, they have much in common: they are based on the assumption that responses are learned or conditioned. The techniques try to reverse the process; in effect, they are methods of unlearning—or perhaps of relearning more normal responses. They are deconditioning techniques.

Recent evidence suggests that these techniques have a common active ingredient when it comes to overcoming phobias effectively: the real-life exposure to the phobia. *The more true-to-life the treatment phobic situation, the more intense the exposure, the longer the exposure lasts at any one time, the more frequently it is repeated, and the more effectively the patient is prevented from making the usual flight or avoidance response, the more quickly and more completely that phobia is overcome.* Of these variables the most important is probably the duration of the exposure. Direct exposures lasting longer than two hours have greater benefit than exposure periods of less than one hour. While almost all books now available to the lay reader on the treatment of anxiety and phobias focus on one or another type of behavior therapy, this is the essence of their approach. It does not mean that the other frills on the various techniques can always be dispensed with. Only that the essential principle of behavior therapy is real-life confrontation of the phobia. If it is followed correctly, the results are often gratifying.

SYSTEMATIC DESENSITIZATION

Systematic desensitization was the first important behavior therapy. If you had a cat phobia, systematic desensitization would lead you through the following sequence: First you would be trained in deep muscle relaxation. Most anxious patients are incapable of doing this effectively at first, and need several hours of training to get their muscles to relax deeply on command. In this state of deep relaxation you would then be asked to visualize vividly seeing a cat about

100 yards away for about 15 seconds. Then you would think of something pleasant and relaxing. Again, you would be asked to think of the same scene for another 10 to 15 seconds, then to switch over to something pleasant and relax deeply.

This pattern would be repeated over and over again until you could visualize the cat in the distance without any anxiety. It would then be repeated with the cat at 90 yards, 80 yards, 70 yards, and so on. You would have to feel comfortable with each stage before moving the cat closer. Finally, you would be able to visualize the cat in your lap without anxiety—indeed, in a state of deep muscle relaxation. After that, a real cat would be brought in, first in a cage at a distance. Very slowly, sometimes over several sessions, the cat would be moved closer until eventually you could actually tolerate it in your lap without anxiety. Your phobia would be cured.

Systematic desensitization stresses *gradual* exposure accompanied by deep muscle relaxation. The exposure is first in imagination and later in reality. It is logical, gentle, and systematic. But it is slow, and because it requires an expert trained in this method, it can be expensive. At the time it was introduced, in 1958, it was a significant advance over other techniques.

FLOODING

Later, a technique called flooding became popular. This dispensed with the relaxation training. You would be quickly asked to visualize the cat all over you, perhaps scratching you, its eyes right up against yours, its hair all over you. The exaggerated imagery would be repeated for long periods until finally you adapted to it, and the cat would not seem so frightening. In effect, you would mentally learn to cope with the worst cat scenes. The real cat is easy to deal with after that.

COGNITIVE RESTRUCTURING

Cognitive restructuring was an intermarriage of some earlier psychological views modified to be consistent with learning or conditioning theories. It was noticed that phobic patients engaged in much negative catastrophic thinking. "I can't do it," "If I go out, I know I'm bound to run into a cat," "The cat will attack me," "I won't be able to deal with the anxiety," and "I know I'll panic," were common trains of thought. The goal of cognitive restructuring is to modify these thinking patterns and replace them with positive, optimistic thoughts.

EXPOSURE TREATMENT

Although the treatments described so far helped different patients to varying degrees, some researchers noticed that the biggest improvement in overcoming a phobia came after the real-life exposure to it. So they dispensed with the gradual buildup, with the relaxation training, with the thinking about it in imagination first, and they ignored the negative thinking. Indeed, they dispensed with all the talking and thinking about it. The slogan for exposure treatment was action—real, direct, intense, prolonged, repeated action—and no escape from it. The result was that many phobias that took months to overcome before were now conquered quickly, sometimes completely within a few hours.

For someone who has only one phobia, and never gets unexpected attacks, exposure is the treatment of choice. The only disadvantage may be that in some cases patients are simply too frightened to cooperate with this method. In those cases, the buildup may need to be slow and gradual. Relaxation training may help the motivation and give patients a sense of control and calm in the midst of danger. In such cases, desensitizing them to the cat gradually in their mind first may pave the way for later cooperation in reality—the old systematic desensitization is applied. For the brave and motivated, direct real-life exposure is the quickest way to extinguish the phobia.

When it comes to treating the anxiety disease, which involves several phobias and unexpected attacks, however, only in a minority of cases does behavior therapy alone help control the disease or its phobic complications. Drug treatments aren't always necessary. However, good results in the short run are often short-lived and disappointing when the unexpected attacks persist. The behavior therapy may help someone to go back into the avoided supermarket or subway again, but he or she may still fear another attack. When unexpected attacks recur with any significant intensity or frequency, the patient will usually revert quickly to avoidance behavior.

Trying to get results with behavior therapy alone in the anxiety disease can be painfully slow. Even when it works, its major effect is on the phobias, which are only one segment of the problem—in fact merely a complication of the original disease. Even if behavior therapy were completely effective against the phobias, it would be misleading to pretend that in dealing with the complications of a disease, you have effectively treated the disease itself. Diabetics frequently get infections as a complication of their diabetes; antibiotics are used to treat this infectious complication effectively. But no one would pretend that antibiotics are an effective treatment for diabetes. The situation is similar with behavior therapies and the phobias that complicate the anxiety disease.

However, after the metabolic core of the disease has been adequately controlled by an effective medicine, the exposure treatments are often quickly effective in dealing with the phobic complications. When used after the medication, they have the bite they lack when used alone.

The first task after effective medication is to identify and measure the severity of the phobias needing this special treatment. The Phobia Scale (see Figure 14, p. 136) may be helpful for this purpose. Alternatively, a list can be made of the main phobias needing treatment. A fear score on a scale of 0 to 10 is given to each phobia at the start. Then they are systematically tackled one at a time. With treatment, the goal is to reduce all scores to zero. It often helps to have someone, perhaps a close family member, assist you. Best of all would be a behavior therapist trained in the correct application of these methods.

Let us say you fear an elevator. You should take off a few hours. First, you find an elevator where you can usefully spend a few hours carrying out the treatment. You might sit outside the elevator and watch others get on and off. Then you might travel one floor with someone you trust when it's not too crowded; then three floors, then four. Each time you do a little more. You keep repeating your success over and over again. When you feel anxious, you do not allow yourself to run away but stick it out. As long as your medication has been properly adjusted, the anxiety will not mushroom or explode into a panic.

In effect, the anxiety will actually be blocked from rising beyond a certain point. When you feel the anxiety beginning to build up, and you start to think, "What if I get a panic?" and you want to run, *don't*. Stand your ground. Relax, let it pass. It won't rise above a certain point. Then it will fade. You'll be standing in the elevator and the anxiety will have passed and gone. You'll be surprised that you are beginning to feel comfortable.

You now stay in the elevator until you are entirely comfortable before stepping out. You repeat this. You go higher in the elevator. Then you start doing it alone. First one floor at a time, then more as your confidence builds. Before long, you find it quite a bit easier—you know you are mastering it at last. Victory is within your grasp. You go through the same process with each phobia. It helps further if you arrange some reward for yourself after each success.

If you find that little spontaneous panics occur and the phobic anxiety explodes into a big attack while following this therapy, it simply means that the dose of medication you are on may not have been adequately adjusted and may be too low. I have been surprised how quickly and easily many patients overcome their phobias with little struggle in this fashion once they put their minds to it and their medication is adjusted correctly, even when they had been disabled by the phobia for years. Overcoming the first few phobias takes the most courage. But with each one conquered, confidence builds and the whole process gets easier.

So, be brave. Take a risk, stand your ground. Let any unpleasant feelings pass by and be patient. Above all, persist. There is truly no reason why you cannot overcome your phobias.

Give sorrow words; the grief that does not speak
Whispers the o'er-fraught heart and bids 't break.

SHAKESPEARE, *Macbeth*

21. *TARGET 3: STRESSES*

Tammy was only eighteen. She was treated correctly with medication for her spontaneous panic attacks; she had behavior therapy for her phobias. But she was not getting better. In some ways she appeared to get worse as she got better. It was all very puzzling. It seemed as if something was holding her back.

The doctor reviewed the steps he had taken: he thought he had made the right choice of medicine, and his experience told him he had correctly regulated the dose. Her spontaneous attacks had stopped, and he had then focused on exposure treatment of her phobias. But his patient seemed to become more restless and agitated as she progressed along what was otherwise a routine path. It didn't fit the usual pattern of response. There must surely be something feeding the anxiety and fanning the flames of anxiety disease.

During the early evaluation sessions, Tammy had denied having any of the obvious life stresses or conflicts that might explain her symptoms persisting after the spontaneous attacks had stopped. She said that if only she could get rid of the symptoms, all would be well.

The doctor decided to seek Tammy's help in solving the mystery. He asked whether, as her condition improved, something had come into sharper focus that had not been so clear at first. Could she think of anything that might be holding her back. At this, she burst into tears. He was a little surprised at the suddenness and intensity of her reaction. He had only been gently inquiring, not at all sure if anything would turn up.

What Tammy then revealed was a fear that if she got better, her grandfather would die. She knew that it sounded silly and superstitious, but she was really worried that her recovery would be bought at the expense of his death.

Over the next half hour, the mystery unfolded. Tammy had been the first of the grandchildren and her grandfather's favorite. They had always had a special, close relationship. They looked alike, and everyone remarked on how much she took after him. In her early teens, when Tammy's panic attacks and spells were well known to the family, her grandfather told her about his own anxiety spells. He had had them since he was a young man, and his life had been changed as a result. He told her he believed he had passed on these genes to her. In a funny way, he said, it was as if part of him lived on in her. Since she admired him, that made Tammy almost proud of her condition. But her grandfather felt guilty about it. He wanted to make up to her for the disadvantage he had given her.

Over the past two years his kidneys had been failing, and in the past two months he had been in a nursing home with kidney failure. The doctor had told the family that he couldn't last much longer. Her parents worried that allowing Tammy to visit him would only upset her and set her back, but she very much wanted to see him again and kiss him good-bye. It was like making final peace with him. She didn't want to give up the funny way he lived inside her; she wanted to keep it, like him, alive. When he died, she knew, something inside her would die a little, too. Then it would also be easier to let the condition die out. She wanted to remember him as her smiling, always benevolent, ever fearless protector. The image of him as an anxious man was not how she perceived him. She could let that part die when he died. But not before.

The doctor listened quietly, attentively. Tammy was pleased he didn't interrupt her; indeed, she was surprised by how respectful his reaction seemed to be. He was taking it all at face value, without judgment, the way she saw it. When she had finished, he told her frankly that he was touched by her story. He suggested that he could speak to her parents and impress on them that it would help rather than hurt if she could visit her grandfather once or twice before he died and while he was still alert. Also, he agreed not to press her to make any further improvements in her symptoms until her grandfather's situation was resolved. Since he knew she didn't want to preserve the image of her grandfather as an anxious, fearful man, he thought that after he died she would be ready to take the final steps toward recovery.

The necessary arrangements were made, and Tammy visited her grandfather twice. He died five weeks later. Within several weeks of his death she felt more at peace again and ready to move on with her life. During their last conversation together, her grandfather had even said that he wanted her to have a life without fear—a thought that she now repeated in her mind and found comforting. He was perceptive to the end in reading her thoughts.

Using psychotherapy to help patients deal with environmental stress involves three important steps. They are first to listen; then to clarify the problem; and finally to support any necessary changes to resolve the problem.

LISTENING

The anxiety disease is a definable, researchable entity. But each victim brings his or her own individuality and flavor to the illness. The special concerns of each patient must be listened to and heard. Frequently, as in Tammy's case, this has a bearing on the outcome. Patients respond best to those who listen to them with respect, accepting what they say at face value, without explaining it away, theorizing, or judging it prematurely. To listen patiently without being judgmental is difficult but important. It is the foundation of effective support.

Respect must be given to the reality of the experience and the symptoms, and to each patient's world. Symptoms cannot be dismissed as being "all in the mind." The reality is that they are very concretely within the body.

CLARIFYING THE PROBLEM

In the process of listening, the problems confronting the patient will emerge more clearly. Sometimes there are stresses that have activated the patient's biological vulnerability. Or there may be current stresses that are aggravating the intensity of the disease. These stresses may also complicate and delay recovery; they may even be robbing the patient of the chance for the best possible improvement. Such stresses, problems, or conflicts need to be identified precisely. And once identified, they need to be clarified.

This calls for reviewing them from all possible angles. As each layer is examined and peeled away, the next layer of the problem becomes more clearly visible. In the process, the various possible solutions to problems are usually reviewed in detail. The advantages and disadvantages of different solutions are examined in a systematic way, so that the issues can be seen clearly. Once again, as with listening, the process is one of clarification without judgment, but with compassion and respect.

During this listening and clarifying process, certain problems turn up with surprising frequency. The patient feels that the whole problem is his fault, that he is to blame for doing this to himself. Often the guilt is fed by the people the patient respects, who misunderstand the disease. They and the patient need to know the patient is not to blame and cannot will it all away. The disease should be seen as being like any other illness one might fall victim to.

Frequent psychological complications include fears that the patient is having a nervous breakdown, losing control, or about to go crazy. Patients are often afraid to tell doctors about some of their symptoms, such as the unreality feelings, for fear of being considered psychotic. The fact is, people with this disease do not go crazy (psychotic) and should not consider themselves weak, inadequate, or inferior any more than if they had any other illness. It is also possible to treat the great majority of them as outpatients without having to admit them to a hospital.

SUPPORTING CHANGES

Once the problems have been clarified, the solutions automatically become clearer. Frequently, the best solutions call for making changes in lifestyle, relationships, or directions. Because every individual knows his or her unique circumstances and pressures best, only he can finally choose which solutions in the balance are best for him. But another trusted person is often needed to discuss these with. The patient expects this person to have common sense, to be realistic, to say no when inappropriate solutions are being pursued.

The best person for this role is someone who on the one hand is a voice of reason and reality, yet on the other hand is sensitive to the individual's unique circumstances. There are no ideal solutions, that person knows; there are no objective rules to impose that are best for everyone. There are only good solutions for each individual.

It is the patient who must make the final choice. Once made, it needs to be respected and supported. The patient feels weak, vulnerable, and anxious in his present situation, yet more fearful that a change may invite further problems. Consequently, he needs support and encouragement to make the necessary changes. The helper lends his strength to the patient until the latter can recover his confidence in himself. For the helper, then, the process is one of listening, clarifying, and giving support. For the patient, the parallel process is to identify the problem, review possible solutions, and finally make the necessary changes.

The fact is that sometimes drugs and behavior therapy alone are just not enough. Interpersonal and psychosocial conflicts may remain after drug treatment and behavior therapy, to delay full recovery or even aggravate the condition. After the first two treatment steps, these problems may come into sharper focus; when the spontaneous attacks and phobias have been overcome, the patient often sees them more clearly. At this point he also has more psychological energy liberated to deal with them. Alongside the development of sophisticated drug and behavioral treatments, and other diagnostic technologies, the importance of compassion, caring, and humanity must not be lost. Some people still just need somebody to talk to.

I many times thought peace had come,
When peace was far away;
As wrecked men deem they sight the land
At centre of the sea,

And struggle slacker, but to prove,
As hopelessly as I,
How many the fictitious shores
Before the harbour lie.

EMILY DICKINSON

22. *TARGET 4: LONG-TERM MANAGEMENT*

The long-range goal in managing the anxiety disease is to prevent or effectively minimize a flare-up of the disease or its complications. The gains that have been achieved in treating biological causes, phobias, and stress have to be maintained. The better the patient understands his or her condition and how best to treat it, the more favorable the long-term outcome will be. Providing adequate information to both patient and family is the best way of achieving this goal. They can then become the doctor's best allies in reducing the chance of relapse and minimizing complications in drug treatment. Knowledge fuels the confidence of the patient on the road to recovery.

If there has been no significant recurrence of any of the spontaneous attacks or spells after six to twelve months, tapering the medicine off very slowly should be considered. Sometimes patients feel ready much sooner for a trial without medication. Others want to continue on medication even after a year of doing well: they fear a recurrence and feel comfortable with the medicine. Perhaps their confidence of going it alone without medication is not yet strong enough. It is usually best to heed these messages. Patients often know when they are ready. Nature has its own momentum; respect for each individual's timing and pace can make all the difference.

Before medication is stopped, it is best to taper the doses off slowly over two or three months. An abrupt stop may result in some withdrawal symptoms or even trigger a rebound of the condition itself. Slow withdrawal is less disruptive. There is nothing significant to be gained from stopping the medicine quickly. One advantage of the slow withdrawal is that if a patient gets a recurrence as the dose is lowered, it is usually milder and more rapidly corrected. Relapses are not uncommon after the medications have been stopped. At least half of all patients may get a recurrence of spontaneous attacks of spells or anxiety within two years of stopping the drug, though it is often difficult to predict in advance which patients this will affect.

A frequent dilemma reported by people treated with medication is an independence-from-drug conflict. Many feel they should be able to do it themselves without medicine. They don't like the idea of needing a pill in order to control these feelings and not being able to do it themselves. These feelings reflect a common need some people have to compete with the medicine to control the disease. At one level it is obviously desirable to be drug-free if one can function well without medicine. However, too frequently patients persist in playing this game even when it is very clear they are getting worse.

Sometimes influential family members who have a mental set against medication perpetuate the problem. There are many reasons for this. One is that the brain and nervous system are still viewed in a different way from the rest of the body; while it is acceptable to treat diseases of the body with medicine, diseases of the nervous system seem different. It is as if people believe the brain should have some unique energy to cure itself. Not too long ago people were reluctant to take any medication, such as an antibiotic, for a severe infection; it was considered unwise to tamper with nature. Such reasoning is still seen in some underdeveloped countries. With time—but only quite recently—we have abandoned the view for practical reasons.

However, the nervous system is the last organ in the body to be seriously invaded by medical science. The social and political upheaval of the 1960s and early 1970s, with its associated drug abuse, further slowed down social acceptance of even helpful medicine that influenced nervous system diseases. Future generations will undoubtedly have a more mature and practical perspective on the issue. In the meantime the most practical approach is for the patient to view the medicine in much the same way as the diabetic patient views his insulin: he knows it is necessary to control his disease, even though he wishes he did not have to take it. He knows how to use it correctly and is familiar with its side effects. Above all, he approaches it practically, in a matter-of-fact fashion, without becoming unnecessarily upset over his need to depend on it. As patients move toward this view over time, they also become more effective in managing their chronic disease.

Since relapses are not uncommon, how to deal with them is the single most important long-term issue. The best way is by early intervention. In general, the more quickly a flare-up is treated, the more effectively it can be controlled and the smaller the chance that there will be any complications or phobias. When a patient has a flare-up, the recurrence of symptoms progresses again through the stages described earlier in this book. In order to prevent the development of phobias, it is usually necessary to control the spells of spontaneous attacks within the first two or three weeks of the recurrence. When treated very early with medication in this way, no one may even notice that there has been a significant change in the patient, and he or she can continue working and functioning normally without again acquiring any disability from the phobias.

Early detection of a relapse is therefore clearly very important. Each patient should learn to identify the relapse aggravators. There are some obvious common aggravators shared by most patients, especially significant stress situations such as the death of a loved one. But the relapse aggravators are by no means all psychological. Others include physical illness of many kinds (even viral infections), anesthesia, surgery, childbirth, and smoking marijuana. Although alcohol may calm the anxiety symptoms for a few hours, several hours after drinking even modest amounts of alcohol, many patients report a rebound flare-up of their symptoms. Drinking coffee and caffeine-containing drinks may worsen the symptoms. Unaccustomed exercise such as taking up jogging or aerobics suddenly have aggravated the symptoms in others, probably by increasing their blood lactate levels. During the premenstrual phase of the menstrual cycle, many women report a flare-up in the frequency and intensity of panic attacks. Frequently these are the last attacks to clear with treatment—and the first to reappear during a recurrence. Some aggravators are very individual. Over time, many patients notice patterns in the things that are likely to trigger a flare-up for them. Knowing these in advance can help them take steps that may enable them to neutralize some of the impact or even avoid it altogether.

One pattern of relapse starts with headaches that become persistent and progressively more resistant to ordinary medication. Then depressed moods may set in, often for no good reason, out of proportion to the reality of the situation. Next, within two or three weeks, spells start in isolation. Finally, these occur in clusters, with panic or anxiety, which eventually leads to more and more phobias.

We have found that patients who have had several relapses over the years learn to identify each relapse sooner as a real relapse and to accept an early intervention with medication. Often the medicine alone is sufficient to treat the relapses. Relapses rarely require behavior therapy since the patients have not yet relearned new phobias.

A SUMMARY OF DIAGNOSIS AND TREATMENT

Figure 19 sums up in a simple diagram the essence of the diagnosis and treatment strategy that has been outlined so far.

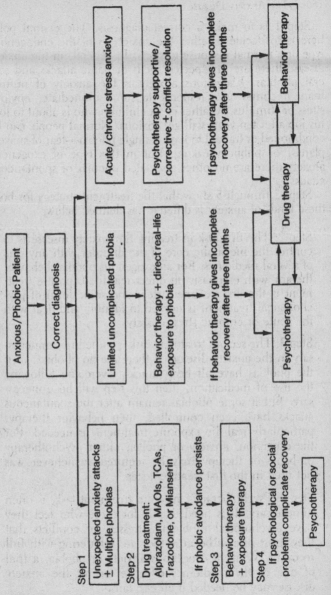

Figure 19. Treatment steps in anxiety disorders

Anxious / Phobic Patient → Correct diagnosis

Step 1

- Unexpected anxiety attacks ± Multiple phobias
- Limited uncomplicated phobia
- Acute / chronic stress anxiety

Step 2

- Drug treatment: Alprazolam, MAOIs, TCAs, Trazodone, or Mianserin
- Behavior therapy + direct real-life exposure to phobia
- Psychotherapy supportive / corrective ± conflict resolution

If phobic avoidance persists

If behavior therapy gives incomplete recovery after three months

If psychotherapy gives incomplete recovery after three months

Step 3

- Behavior therapy + exposure therapy
- Psychotherapy ⇄ Drug therapy ⇄ Behavior therapy

Step 4

If psychological or social problems complicate recovery

- Psychotherapy

Step 1 is to make a correct diagnosis. The central point here is to decide whether the anxiety is of the endogenous type or a normal response to stress. In general, in the anxiety disease there are unexpected spells or panic attacks and several phobias. Exogenous anxiety is the anxiety of normal man: it comes as a response to some immediate, obvious stress or stimulus. A father of six children who is about to lose his job after ten years will get anxious. Normal people can be conditioned or trained to have a single phobia—fear of snakes, planes, or public speaking. But in this type of exogenous anxiety there are no other associated phobias or spontaneous attacks.

Steps 2 through 5 show that the treatment strategy for both these kinds of anxiety is different, as defined below:

Step 2: The first task in treating the anxiety disease is to control the metabolic core of the disorder with any one of several medicines. For an exogenous phobia, behavior therapy with emphasis on direct real-life exposure treatment is the first treatment step, and some form of psychological treatment is needed to identify and deal with the acute or chronic stress anxiety.

Step 3: The second treatment task is sometimes unnecessary in the anxiety disease. If there are no phobias, or if the phobias have all been quickly overcome following the use of medication, then this step will be unnecessary. But if some phobias remain after the spontaneous attacks have been controlled, then behavior therapy, particularly real-life exposure treatment, is needed. For the exogenous anxiety or phobia, either psychotherapy or behavior therapy may be required—whichever was not used in the first treatment step.

Step 4: Psychotherapy, the third treatment task, is often unnecessary. It is needed only for those who feel they have psychosocial problems, stresses, or conflicts that they must discuss because they are interfering with full recovery. With an exogenous anxiety or phobia, a trial of one of the medicines effective against the anxiety disease may be needed if all else fails.

Step 5: This involves long-term management, and requires monitoring progress, side effects of medication, and complications. It calls for maintaining consistent improvement against the first three treatment targets.

23. *THE FAMILY*

The life of an entire family is severely affected when one member has the anxiety disease, and the support of that family can play a crucial role in long-term recovery.

Mrs. Gallo had several members of her family come in with her to the doctor's office. She felt more secure with them, but she also felt ashamed that she needed such an entourage and was so dependent. Dr. De Vere's office was quite crowded; her husband and two older children came, as did her sister, her mother, and her sister-in-law. Her father had refused to appear. To go to the doctor with a problem like this was an admission of weakness, he said, and a mental weakness at that; it was also an acknowledgment that the family had not been able to deal with the problem, which was a dishonor. She needed to show more courage and exercise more willpower.

Mrs. Gallo's mother began by blaming herself for the entire problem. She felt very guilty for all the things she had done wrong as a mother. She knew she could not have brought up her daughter correctly. She had wanted her to be a well-behaved, obedient, God-fearing Catholic girl. The psychologists in their new books on child rearing obviously disapproved of several things she had done. If she had the opportunity to start over, she said, she would do it differently.

Mr. Gallo picked up on this and claimed that he too was partly to blame for not always being the best of husbands. Sometimes with the stress of working, providing for everyone, and doing many of the household chores, he escaped into drink, which upset his wife even more. But twelve years was a long time to have to put up with this kind of problem, and it was hard on him, too. His coworkers kidded him about doing the grocery shopping, asking him whether his wife made him cook the meals too. Because of her fears, he couldn't bring his wife to the big annual dance or even to any family get-togethers. They had no social life at all.

Of course it affected all the children as well, and the two who had come along added their piece. They had an extra burden to carry that other kids didn't, since their mother could never bring them to school, meet with the teachers, or even come to graduations.

At this point Mrs. Gallo began to cry, claiming she was the real one at fault. She had missed out on a large part of her family life because of her problem, but it had the better of her. Sometimes she wanted to give up, since no matter how hard she tried she couldn't seem to cope with it. Maybe she would be better off dead, leaving her husband to find another woman who would make him a more normal wife and the children a better mother.

The family had several questions for the doctor; for example, they wondered how much Mrs. Gallo could be helped, how much of her condition was just stress, whether it was a mental problem, and whether she was having a nervous breakdown that would require hospitalization.

The life of the entire family is indeed strained and disrupted by this anxiety disease. Everyone involved deserves great credit just for putting up with the patient's symptoms and for readjusting their lives to cope with the restrictions imposed on them.

Children have to learn not to depend on their parents as

much as other children do. Although they come to see their parent's problem as a limitation on their lives, they also learn that they shouldn't take it personally.

Parents of people with this disease feel guilty and blame themselves for not raising their children properly. And spouses have to carry many extra burdens: they must be part mother as well as father, to fill in for what the affected parent cannot do. Their lives are also restricted.

But it is all especially hard on the victims. They are blamed for a weakness and they feel weak. Yet they know they cannot will the disease away. They feel guilty for what they cannot do. They become depressed about the life they are missing, aware that it is slipping away from them. They feel hopeless, helpless, and worthless.

It is actually remarkable how few families break up under the strain of all this, and it is to everyone's credit that they all try to help make the best of a bad situation. For the fact is that no one is to blame, so no one should feel guilty. The anxiety disease is not a form of craziness, nor is it just "all in the patient's mind." Victims rarely need hospitalization; many manage well as outpatients.

Dr. De Vere explained that what Mrs. Gallo had was an illness now recognized as the anxiety disease, the focus of much recent intensive study. Just as you wouldn't blame someone for having high blood pressure or diabetes, it also made no sense to blame Mrs. Gallo for having the anxiety disease. For it couldn't simply be willed away, any more than diabetes can be. Stress and conflict don't cause the condition, though they can aggravate it just as they can aggravate problems with diabetes.

He recommended that her treatment start with a course of anti-panic medicine. When it began to work, the entire family could be helpful in getting her to go out again, encouraging her to do things she had avoided doing, and generally getting her to stand her ground and become more independent. It would be much easier to do this after several weeks on the medication.

He said that they would all have to make other readjustments as Mrs. Gallo got better and felt more independent and assertive again. But adjusting to these gradual improvements would be easier than what the family had already been through in the course of her illness.

The elder daughter looked worried. When the doctor questioned her, she said uneasily that she didn't want her mother to be dependent on drugs, like a junkie. Dr. De Vere acknowledged her concern while agreeing that many families were certainly worried about the use of such drugs. But he went on to explain that psychiatry has become more sophisticated in the use of a wide range of medications. Nowadays many drugs with quite specific effects work without leaving the patient looking drugged or drunk.

The story of the Gallo family captures the fears and concerns, conflicts and stresses experienced by the families of anxiety disease victims. Such a family is often beset by shame and guilt, confused by misapprehensions, and full of regrets at missed opportunities. But there are even more cases where the family forms a powerful bond as its members struggle together to cope with a force of nature they can neither understand nor control. It is a tale of quiet fortitude and courage that too often goes untold.

Part Five _____
THE PHASES
OF RECOVERY

What wound did ever heal but by degrees?

SHAKESPEARE, _Othello_

> *Our doubts are traitors*
> *And make us lose the good we oft might win*
> *By fearing to attempt.*
>
> SHAKESPEARE, *Measure for Measure*

24. *PHASE 1: DOUBT*

Maria and Adam had just left the doctor's office after a lengthy consultation with him. What she had been told made Maria feel as if she was walking around in a daze. One part of her was relieved; another part was overjoyed at the possibility of getting better. But she also felt frightened at what lay ahead. Her heart was beating faster. She was depressed that her problem had gone so long untreated, and annoyed that she had not been told all this before and it had not been managed properly. Yet she was happy that finally something was being done so that she could live normally again.

She told Adam that it was as if she had been a prisoner for years in a nameless prison, for an undesignated crime she had tried in vain to identify, with an uncertain future, surrounded by people who failed to appreciate her helplessness. Then one day without explanation someone had stepped out of the crowd and announced that she would be released from prison, that there was no crime, and that she would enjoy full freedom again. Was it any wonder that a series of conflicting emotions was surging through her mind?

At the doctor's office she had been asked to complete some questionnaires and scales in the hour before seeing him. It surprised her to find all of her symptoms listed one after another on the pages of the scales she was completing. Obviously someone saw that all these apparently diverse symptoms striking various parts of the body were connected together in some way. There must be many other people who had a similar pattern of symptoms; the forms hadn't been printed up just for her.

She was also surprised by how much the doctor knew about the condition, and even more surprised to learn there were doctors who specialized in treating it. His questions and his way of describing the symptoms told her that he was on her wavelength and that he understood. His insight into the condition saved her from having to explain much of what others had misunderstood. His calm confidence throughout the interview and in discussing the treatment was reassuring. She wanted to follow his directions and agree to his plan of treatment, but she could sense her own helplessness and dependence in this acquiescence. She felt drawn to the protection that radiated from his confidence; she was also frightened by her vulnerability to it.

Later, Maria became filled with doubts. She told Adam she wasn't sure whether to believe all the doctor had said. After all, wouldn't some other doctor of the many she had seen have suggested this course of action earlier? His views seemed to be the opposite of what most people had been telling her for years. He didn't think all these symptoms were in her mind, but sometimes she wondered if they really were; how could she tell the difference? Perhaps she hadn't told him the whole story properly. For example, she had forgotten to tell him about that numbness she got in her face sometimes. Maybe he had made a mistake and only thought he knew what was wrong with her; maybe he was mixing it up with something very similar. She knew well enough how many diseases her condition could imitate.

Adam, however, was impressed with the doctor's grasp of the problem. He suggested that they go and pick up the medicine. But after they had fetched it, Maria panicked again. What if it didn't work? She would just be putting up with a lot of side effects for nothing. Besides, she had had the condition for so long it probably was too far gone to treat by now. Sometimes things got so ingrained they were irreversible.

Adam suggested that she take the first pill right away. Still she vacillated, protesting that she ought to check the whole thing out a little more, perhaps get another opinion. She insisted on reading the package insert that came with the bottle carefully, and checking out the medication in some of her books. After all, it was her body that was consuming it. This stuff could really harm her. Adam reminded her that the doctor had gone over all the details of the side effects in the office and had been very explicit about how best to deal with them. And so it continued. They went back and forth on the issue for the rest of the day with few intermissions.

When Maria did finally take in the side effects listed on the package, they frightened her even more. There was something about seeing it all written down in black and white that was devastating. Adam simply couldn't believe what was happening. For years she had been crying, "Help," saying she would agree to anything that would give her relief and get her back to normal. Now here she was with much of the solution quite literally in the palm of her hand—and she couldn't take the first step.

The next evening when they met again, she still had not started the medicine. She had spent all day in the library reading medical books and had even gone to the trouble of checking out her doctor's credentials, consulting with some other friends and a few doctors on the phone. She couldn't find a good reason not to go ahead, but she still had a lot of questions.

By now Maria could see better what was happening. She was frightened that taking the medicine was an admission of weakness on her part, an acknowledgment that she couldn't control the fear in her mind herself. This left her feeling somewhat ashamed and guilty. Yet . . . it was also frightening to think that there might be a disease that couldn't be controlled mentally, that could strike fear into you at will.

Further, taking the medication was an admission of defeat psychologically in a way, and she feared that the terror demon might take advantage of this surrender and grow larger.

Then, if the drug didn't work, it would really have her. She was afraid of being on medicine for a long time, and in a way she was even frightened of getting better. It had been so long since she felt normal, she didn't know whether she could handle being normal again. She had grown to fear anything different or unfamiliar, and an ordinary life now would feel extremely strange. Being panicky was more familiar.

Maria went back to visit her doctor with all her questions. She worried that he would be unhappy with her doubts and fears, but he seemed content to review them systematically and patiently with her. In fact, he encouraged her to write down all her questions between visits and bring the list to him, so he could answer them for her. He gave her a side effects checklist for her to record systematically any that she experienced between visits so they could review them thoroughly. He told her many patients with this disease feared medication and starting treatment; such doubts and procrastinations were part of the process. You just had to accept it, be patient with it, but also be persistent in overcoming it.

She could sense in him an incredible persistence. He had no fear of this fear disease. Indeed, she could see that he took pleasure in the struggle. Finally, Maria asked one last favor: she would start the medicine the next morning if she could come to his office and take the first tablet in his waiting room, then stay there a few hours to be sure she was all right. She realized it was a silly request, but she knew it would make it easier for her.

She was relieved to learn not only that it was all right to take the pill there, but that another patient was coming in the next day for just the same purpose. The doctor agreed to introduce them so they could go through it together, and to check on both of them from time to time. She wasn't alone!

Maria was started on imipramine. The side effects disrupted her quite a bit at first; however, she was coming to see these more as friendly guides to the correct effective dose and less as dangerous assassins. With time she learned better how to distinguish between the real side effects of the drug and the symptoms of her condition. She knew she shouldn't expect any real benefit until she had been on a therapeutic dose for at least three weeks.

She did feel strong flare-ups of doubt during those weeks.

Perhaps this was all a mistake . . . perhaps she couldn't get better . . . perhaps one or another side effect would really harm her. The first three weeks was a bumpy road. She counted the days. On the twenty-first day she woke up, expecting this to be the day it would work. But nothing seemed any different. She still felt anxious, she still had a few spikes of symptoms. At lunch she had a choking spell and got dizzy. She was short of breath, her heart raced; she could feel herself getting more hysterical. She called Adam at work and told him she was going to stop the medicine. It wasn't working and it was taking too much out of her.

By evening Adam had calmed her down, persuading her that the doctor had not promised results in exactly twenty-one days. She was still wretched, though. The disease tossed her between periods of hysteria and moments of calm insight into the whole thing; it was like being driven mad, but being allowed to watch herself doing so at the same time. But she realized now that her doubts had been a way of coping with the fear of facing something new and unfamiliar. And she resolved to try to be brave. She wouldn't give up yet.

> —*I pray you, give her air,*
> *Gentlemen, this queen will live. Nature awakes;*
> *A warmth breathes out of her.*
> *. . . See how she [be]gins*
> *To blow into life's flower again!*

SHAKESPEARE, Pericles

25. PHASE 2: MASTERY

The next morning Maria lay in bed at dawn in that dreamy state between sleep and wakefulness. She kept drifting in and out peacefully. She heard the birds singing outside her window and got lost in how pleasant the sounds were. A little later her clock radio came on as it did every morning to the sounds of the local classical music station. She lay there listening to a performance of Chopin's Second Piano Concerto. What a great performance, she thought. She couldn't remember ever having heard it better played. It was positively magical.

She drifted off to sleep again, and was woken later by the phone ringing. It was Adam, with an invitation to join him and some other couples from work for dinner. She agreed without hesitating.

While making breakfast, she was humming one of her favorite songs. All of a sudden it dawned on her that today she really *did* feel different. She hadn't experienced any anxiety on waking up. Things seemed more pleasurable—the birds singing, the classical music. The Chopin she judged so outstanding was the same as the one in her own collection. She was even humming.

That dark cloud of despair that had hung over her for so long just was not there. Today everything seemed a little richer. Then she realized that she had agreed without hesitation to go out to eat with a group of people in a strange restaurant and had promptly forgotten about it. Two weeks before, the idea would have panicked her and she would never have agreed. It was a frightening thought. After all, the past several times she had tried, she had had to leave in a panic. As she thought more about all this, she wondered whether she should call Adam and back out of it. But although she was apprehensive now, she was feeling so good that she decided to risk it and go. Her doctor had told her that once the drug took effect, the anxiety would be blocked from rising beyond a certain acceptable point. It wouldn't mushroom explosively as it usually did. At this point going back into the situations she had previously avoided would help her to overcome her fears. She was almost curious to see what would happen.

By the time Adam picked her up, Maria was beginning to worry about how well the day had gone for her. Could it last? She was a little apprehensive on her way to the restaurant. She felt that old what-if anxiety: What if she got a spell there? Would it set her back? But it wasn't as strong as usual.

Adam was in a positively charming mood. She was soon talking of other things. They were a lively group at dinner; she found herself really caught up in the fun of the evening, enjoying company in a way she hadn't done for years. Adam was so surprised throughout the evening at her good humor, he was almost afraid to comment on it. He couldn't help noticing that her face was less strained than usual, her facial muscles more relaxed. Later that evening Maria told him that she still couldn't believe she had got through the rest of the evening without even a twinge of a spell. She put her head on his shoulder and embraced him gently for a long time. Life was coming back to her.

In the weeks that followed, Maria and Adam worked together at overcoming her phobias. He would first travel one stop in the subway with her, then two, then three. Then he would have her go ahead one stop in the train and wait in the station; he caught up with her in the next train. With repetition she managed to go further and further alone, and she experienced less apprehension and difficulty. They did the same thing with elevators and driving on highways. In crowded shopping malls she tried a little at first with him, then spent more and more time there not knowing where he was in the mall. A few times she experienced surges of anticipatory anxiety, but then she could feel these surges literally blocked physically somewhere between her chest and stomach. Realizing that the anxiety was now prevented from rising out of control made her more confident to try more. Her confidence fed on itself. She was really mastering her problem at every level.

> *When the sun shineth,*
> *make hay.*
>
> JOHN HEYWOOD, *Proverbs 1546*

26. *PHASE 3: INDEPENDENCE*

Maria looked wonderful: she was taking better care of herself and felt more attractive. She was happier, more confident, and less fearful with each passing week. The spark and bubble had come back into her life. She felt stronger and more effective in dealing with others; she was coping with things differently now.

She appreciated life more and wanted to live it more intensely. She involved herself in new activities and responsibilities. Her emotions and feelings were stronger, as if someone had turned up the volume on them—she wasn't going to be anyone's doormat any more, wasn't going to take stress from anyone. She didn't fear people in authority any more and her feelings for Adam were stronger; but she also felt attracted to other men and thought more about dating them.

In fact, Maria didn't stop much to reflect. She felt like a prisoner who had just been released from a long jail term: she had a fresh start. She wanted to catch up on everything she had missed. The prospect excited her and she was euphoric about getting better.

Adam's reaction was less euphoric, his feelings somewhat more mixed. He was pleased she was recovering well. But she was behaving a little differently. She was more aggressive and assertive with him 'and others if they differed with her. This led to some embarrassing conflicts for her at work and with some of her old friends. She was more demanding. When anyone pointed this out to her, she would accuse them of preferring her weak, passive, fearful, and sick again. That, she announced, was out of the question. She was more independent now.

But there was a wild streak in this striving for independence and freedom. Adam was worried at how much Maria was taking on: she was redecorating her apartment, buying more clothes, had bought a new car, and wanted to be out every night. She had become more uninhibited, less shy; there was a certain callousness and lack of sensitivity to others in her behavior. At times she even appeared to be flirting with some of his friends, which left him feeling jealous. Yet in other ways their life together was happier and fuller than it had ever been. He wished, though, that she could be a little less euphoric and less stridently independent, and that she would consider the consequences to others of her behavior at times. It was like parenting an enthusiastic adolescent—at once delightful and worrisome to observe. But you had to accommodate it and hope it wouldn't get out of hand.

> *When I thought I had all the answers,*
> *They changed all the questions.*

POSTER CAPTION

27. *PHASE 4: READJUSTMENT*

In the fairytale liberation from the bondage of disease, everything begins to seem possible. The patient feels she has found the answer to her prayers.

In time, however, the practical complications of everyday life begin to impose themselves once more on the dream of liberation and independence. Unexpected problems arise, demanding new answers. Unanticipated readjustments must be made as the patient reenters the mainstream of life.

Just as Maria was in the full bloom of her independence, when the solutions seemed clear and the possibilities limitless, other realities required her to make such adjustments.

In a moment of exuberance, Maria decided to organize a surprise birthday party for Adam. Now that she had been on the medicine a few months and had overcome her phobias, she felt up to it. Besides, she knew how much Adam would appreciate it. The party was a great success. Maria was delighted to be able to mix socially with so many people again and proud she had taken it on herself to organize the party.

But that night while driving home, Adam was involved in a car crash. His family called to say he was in critical condition. When she got to the hospital, it was worse than she expected. Adam was in a coma. He had a fractured leg and head injuries. He was on a respirator to keep him breathing. The only sign of life was the little blip spiking away quietly on the heart monitor with each heartbeat. His family was extremely upset, all in tears. Maria was overcome herself, but could see that she was actually coping better than the others.

Over the next three days, Maria spent as much time as possible at Adam's bedside. She also went out of her way to help his family, supporting them, trying to give them hope. Because she was so busy, Maria realized she was skipping some of her scheduled doses of medication.

Then the inevitable happened: she had a panic attack right there in the hospital. Her heart started racing out of control; she felt she was getting dizzy and about to faint. She feared she might lose consciousness, perhaps even slip into a coma. It was very frightening. Increasingly she was also haunted by her behavior of the last few months. In the euphoria of getting better she had not stopped to consider others very much; in so many ways, she hadn't been thoughtful enough. She hadn't stopped to reflect. Life had become a little unreal and she had almost forgotten how much Adam meant to her. These were realities to consider.

On the fourth day, while Maria was sitting beside Adam's bed alone and lost in thought, she felt a hand squeeze hers. It was Adam's. She looked closely: he was coming out of the coma. Gradually, Adam began to recover. It would be several weeks before he could walk again, but in a curious way the accident brought them closer together. In helping Adam, Maria felt she could repay him for all he had done for her through her illness. Because he was vulnerable and needed her support now, she felt less ashamed about her dependency and weakness during her own illness. Besides, it was good to feel needed and appreciated. She regretted how much she had displaced Adam in her quest for independence. She realized she must choose independence with responsibility rather than rebellion without sensitivity. She, too, was recovering.

* * *

It is important to see the phases of recovery as a process, to view them as a part of nature's way rather than judging them as "good" or "bad." When the patient's behavior and the reactions of family and friends toward it are accepted as natural phases of the recovery process rather than actions to be judged, the recovery is easier to understand and to facilitate, without any unnecessary interference. Helping the participants to stand back and view it in this light lessens their chance of being ensnared in the process and promotes better transition through each phase.

It is sometimes necessary to make changes. And both the victim and the family may need to readjust to these changes that occur as part of getting better. Some catching up psychologically may be necessary. Patients often become less passive and more assertive, and move from being very dependent to becoming more independent. Sometimes relationships need adjusting to accommodate these changes. Sometimes those who helped the patient most during the crippling stages of the anxiety disease now feel the most cast aside—no longer needed or appreciated. It is necessary for the recovering patient to be aware of this and to help his or her former supporter during the transition.

Because all kinds of things that were impossible before now become possible, patients often start formulating new goals for their lives—perhaps going back to school, or fulfilling longed-for dreams. Sooner or later most patients see that they must make changes to reenter the mainstream of life, and in the process they must be thoughtful and attentive to the feelings of those close to them. Sometimes it requires a jolt to impress these everyday practical realities into their sense of liberation from chronic captivity. Adam's accident had such an effect on Maria. Often the passage of time and the realities of daily living are enough to force it on the patient's attention.

As they move through the recovery phases, patients still need much encouragement and support. Although their improvement is more dramatic in the first few months of treatment, there is progressive healing over a much longer period of time with medication. Occasionally full recovery can be quite protracted. Their improvements call for rewards and words of praise. Family and friends must be patient and provide room for the normal mistakes and flounderings of growth as the patient seeks a more secure footing once again on the road of life.

Maria had allowed herself to skip her medication as she grew confident in her recovery. This, combined with the sudden stress of Adam's accident, allowed her disease to reactivate. Patients need to learn to have a realistic outlook on this illness. They need to accept the fact that they actually have it, that it will require careful long-term monitoring and effective treatment if and when it recurs.

Sometimes the anxiety disease fades out and the patient manages for years without medicine. But the vulnerability to it is always there. Should it recur, it has to be treated quickly and effectively, and the doses taken correctly rather than in inadequate quantities. With such a realistic and practical outlook, it is possible to live with this disease and yet maintain a positive outlook.

THE FUTURE

The future is hopeful. More has been learned about this disorder in the last fifteen years than in all the century before. In the past few years the pace has visibly quickened. Old views are being revised; the idea that it is an illness rather than a state of mind or a response to stress is attracting more interest and gaining more credibility. This model offers new hope when compared with older models that invoke stress, conflicts, or conditioning alone. It suggests a whole new way of researching one of man's most enduring and common disorders. It invites us to study the disease as we have every other disease—scientifically, medically, and biochemically. It provides a framework to integrate this with the older stress and conditioning views.

There is little doubt that in the near future this model will help us better to unravel the mysteries of the anxiety disease, and will lead us to a better understanding of its causes. It will help us find more accurate laboratory tests to aid us in diagnosing it. Above all, it will guide us to newer, safer, more rapid and effective treatments. We have already come a long way in controlling it. The rest is only a matter of time.

FURTHER READING

All of the books listed contain extensive reference sections for those who wish to explore further. Many present one treatment perspective. This author does not necessarily endorse all their recommendations. They reflect the best of a wide range of viewpoints, by acknowledged experts in the field, often in disagreement with each other. *The Anxiety Disease* may help the reader to place the differing viewpoints in perspective.

Fann, W. E.; Karacan, I.; Porkorny, A. D.; and Williams, R.L. *Phenomonology and Treatment of Anxiety.* New York: Springer Medical Scientific Books, 1979.

Klein, D. F.; Gittleman, R.; Quitkin, F.; and Rifkin, A. *Diagnosis and Drug Treatment of Psychiatric Disorders: Adults and Children.* Baltimore: Williams Wilkins, 1980. This is a classic in modern psychiatry. Written for psychiatrists, it is a gold mine of information on the range of drug treatments available in modern psychiatry and how to use them correctly. The first author is a pioneer in medical psychiatry.

————, and Rabkin, J. G., eds. *Anxiety: New Research and Changing Concepts.* New York: Raven Press, 1981. This is a valuable collection of papers by experts, reflecting the changing concepts on anxiety and anticipating future trends. Written for psychiatrists, it contains the best of the biological viewpoint.

Lader, M. H., and Marks, I. M. *Clinical Anxiety*. London: Heinemann Medical, 1971.

Marks, I. M. *Fears and Phobias*. New York: Academic Press, 1969. This was the principal reference book on the diagnosis and classification, and the behavioral and psychological treatments, of fears and phobias during the 1970s. It was a very influential book that set the stage for much of the subsequent research in this area.

————. *Living with Fear*. New York: McGraw-Hill, 1978.

————. *Cure and Care of the Neuroses: the Theory and Practice of Behavioral Psychotherapy*. New York: Wiley, 1981. *Living with Fear* (above) was written for a lay audience, while this is the more technical version of the same ideas written for experts. Marks has been a pioneer in the behavioral approaches to phobias and his work embodies the best of the behavioral views on anxiety and phobia.

Mathews, A. M.; Gelder, M. G.; and Johnston, D. W. *Agoraphobia: Nature and Treatment*. New York: Guilford Press, 1981. A technical overview of behavior therapies for agoraphobia.

Mavisakalian, M.; and Barlow, D. *Phobia: Psychological and Pharmacological Treatment*. New York: Guilford Press, 1981. An overview of psychological and drug treatments for agoraphobia. The biological and drug treatments are underrepresented.

Sheehan, D. V. "Panic Attacks and Phobias." *New England Journal of Medicine* 307 (1982): 156–58. This is a brief overview of some basic assumptions about this disorder and how to treat it, using a medical illness model.

————. "Current Perspectives in the Treatment of Panic and Phobia Disorders." *Drug Therapy* (September 1982). A succinct overview of treatment strategies for anxiety and phobic disorders with special reference to the newer psychotropic drugs.

————, and Claycomb, J. B. "The Use of MAO Inhibitors in Clinical Practice." In *Psychiatric Medicine Update*, edited by J. C. Manschreck. Holland: Elsevier, 1984. A cookbook guide on how to use the MAO inhibitors. These are among the most effective drugs for this disorder, although troublesome to use correctly.

Weekes, C. Peace from Nervous Suffering. New York: Hawthorn Books, 1972.

————. Simple and Effective Treatment of Agoraphobia. New York: Hawthorn Books, 1976. This and Peace from Nervous Suffering (above) are clear, simply written books on agoraphobia for a lay audience. The most easily read of all the books listed, they are reassuring. The treatment sections are somewhat outdated.

Wender, P. H., and Klein, D. F. Mind, Mood and Medicine. New York: Farrar, Straus, Giroux, 1981. This may be the best and most current presentation of the biological and medical orientation to psychiatric disorders for the lay audience. It embodies the best of what modern psychiatry has to offer victims of these diseases.

Wolpe, J. The Practice of Behaviour Therapy. New York: Pergamon Press, 1969. One of the first good books on how to do behavior therapy by an early pioneer in those treatments. Much of what is considered novel today in behavior therapies was described or anticipated by Wolpe in the 1950s and 1960s.

INDEX

acute intoxication, 112
agoraphobia, 45, 59, 60
alcoholic beverages, 69–70, 112
alcoholism, 69–70, 112
alprazolam, 120–22, 126
amitriptyline, 120
anorexia nervosa, 69
anticipated anxiety attacks, 51–52, 52–53, 90
appetite, 69
association, 88, 89–90
atropine, 45
avoidance behavior, 46. See also phobias
avoidance training, 92–93

balance, 19–20
barbiturates, 70
behavior therapy, 107, 128
  cognitive restructuring, 146

exposure treatment, 146–48
  flooding, 145; systematic desensitization, 144–45
belladonna, 45
biochemical abnormalities, 83–85
biological disorders, 81–86
breathing difficulty, 21–22
brucellosis, 109

carcinoid syndrome, 44
cardiac neurosis, 24, 42
castration anxiety, 96
chest pain, 24–25
chest pressure, 24–25
children, and anxiety, 95–96; and fear, 71–73
choking sensation, 25–26
classical conditioning, 87–90
claustrophobia, 60
cognitive restructuring, 146

colitis, spastic, 29
colon. See irritable colon syndrome;
  see also spastic colon syndrome
conditioning, classical, 87–90;
  interoceptive, 94
conversion hysteria, 43

DaCosta, Jacob, 24
DaCosta's Syndrome, 24, 42
delusions, 109
depersonalization, 30–32
depression, 62–65; endogenous, 63;
  symptoms of, 67
derealization, 30–31, 32
desensitization. See systematic
  desensitization
desipramine, 119–120
De Vere, Dr., 162–65
diagnosis, 108–17, 58–60; of anxiety
  disease, 109–12; of medical
  illness, 108–9; with Patient-rated
  Anxiety Scale, 113–17; of
  psychosis, 109
diarrhea, 28–29
Dickinson, Emily, 155
Disability Scale, 135, 138
dizzy spells, 19
Don Quixote, 54
doubts, 169–73
drug abuse, 69–70
drug withdrawal, 109
drugs, adjustment of dose, 123,
  126–127; educating patient
  about, 127–29; fear of, 165,
  170–73; for lactate sensitivity,
  84–85; monitoring response to,
  130–32; monitoring side effects
  of, 135, 139–141; selection of,
  118–21

eating habits, 69
endogenous anxiety, 9–10
endogenous depression, 67
environmental stress, 77, 79,
  97–99, 151
epilepsy, 72, 109
exogenous anxiety, 9, 112
exposure treatment, 146–48

fainting spells, 19
fear, in children, 71–73
flooding, 145
Freud, Sigmund, 75, 78–79, 96
frightened children, 71–73
future, 182–83

Gallo, Mrs., 162–65
Global Improvement Scale, 130–32
globus hystericus, 43
guilt, 64

hallucinations, 109
headaches, 29
heredity, 81–83
Herophilus, 118
high arousal regression, 94–96
Horace, 103
hot flashes, 27
hyperventilation syndrome, 44
hypochondriasis, 39–49
hysteria, 45, 46
hysterical symptoms, 43, 46

idiopathic hypoglycemia, 44
illness phobias, 60
imbalance, 19–20
imipramine, 120, 172
impulse anxiety, 95
independence phase, 177–78
inheritance pattern, 81–83
insomnia, 66–67; terminal, 67
interoceptive conditioning, 94
irritable colon syndrome, 29

Kierkegaard, Soren, 1

lactate sensitivity, 84–85
learning by association, 88, 89
Librium, 70
lightheadedness, 19
locus coeruleus, 85
longevity, 104

manic depression, 109
MAO inhibitors, 85, 119, 120,
  122–23
maprotiline, 120

mastery phase, 174–76
Medlars, 104
Medline, 104
Ménière's disease, 43
models of anxiety, 77–79
monitoring patient, attacks, 132–34; disability, 135, 138; overall improvement, 130–32; phobias, 134, 136–37; side effects, 135, 139–41; symptoms, 132
monoamine oxidase inhibitors. *See* MAO inhibitors.
mortality rate, 104–5
multiple sclerosis, 109

nausea, 27–28
neurasthenia, 67
neurological disorders, 109
nightmares, 67
night panic, 67

palpitations, 22–24
panic attacks, 33–38, 46; frequency of, 35; at night, 67; symptoms of, 34; and tight clothing, 36
paresthesias, 26
Pasternak, Boris, 77
Patient-rated Anxiety Scale, 113–17
Pavlov, 88, 95
pavor nocturnus, 67
petit mal epilepsy, 72
Petrova, 95
phenelzine, 119, 123, 126
pheochromocytoma, 44, 109
Phobia Scale, 147
phobias, 14; agoraphobia, 58–60; and anxiety, 51–53; behavior therapy for, 143–48; claustrophobia, 60; development of, 50–52, 88–90; high arousal regression and, 94–96 illness, 60; limited, 50–53; monitoring, 134, 136–37; the ripple effect and, 91; social, 45, 54–56, 59, 60
phobic avoidance, 57–61
Phobic neurosis, 45
"phobophobia," 59

Pitts, Ferris, 84
P.M.S. (premenstrual syndrome), 18
psychiatrists, 127–28
psychological forces, 87–89
psychologists, 127–28
psychopharmacologists, 127
psychosis, 109
psychotherapy, 107, 151, 160

readjustment phase, 179–82
recovery phase, 179–82
Redmond, Dr. Eugene, 85
regression, high arousal, 94–96
relapse, 157–58
research, 117
reward learning, 92

schizophrenia, 112
security blankets, 93
separation anxiety, 95
sexual anxiety, 68–69
Shakespeare, William, 15, 17, 101, 149, 167, 169
Shelley, Percy Bysshe, 3
Skinner, B.F., 92
sleep patterns, 66–67; excessive sleep, 67; insomnia, 66–67
sleeping tablets, 70
social phobias, 45, 54–56, 59, 60
spastic colitis. *See* colitis
spastic colon syndrome, 45
spells, 17–32; breathing difficulty during, 21–22; chest pain during, 24–25; choking sensation during, 25–26; depersonalization and, 31–32; derealization and, 30–32; diarrhea during, 28–29; dizzy, 19; headaches during, 29; hot flashes during, 27; imbalance during, 19–20; nausea during, 27–28; numbness sensations during, 26; palpitations during, 22–24; symptoms of, 19–32
spontaneous anxiety attacks, 52–53, 88–90
stranger anxiety, 95

stress, 13; environmental, 97–99;
fear and, in children, 73;
reactive, 9, 112; treatment for,
149–54
systematic desensitization, 144–45

terminal insomnia, 67
tetracyclic antidepressants, 119, 122
thyrotoxicosis, 44, 109
tranquilizers, 70, 105, 106
trazodone, 120
treatment, 105–7; drug, *see* drugs;
family and, 162–65; fear of,
171–73; long-term management

and, 155–58; strategy for,
106–7, 158–61; for stress,
149–54; targets of, 105–7
triazolobenzodiazepine, 85
triazolopyridine, 122
tricyclic antidepressants, 85, 119,
120, 122
studies, 83
tyramine, 119

Valium, 70
vertigo hysterique, 43

women, anxiety disease and, 11–13

ABOUT THE AUTHOR

DAVID V. SHEEHAN, M.D. was Director of Anxiety Research of the Department of Psychiatry at Massachusetts General Hospital, and Assistant Professor of Psychiatry at Harvard Medical School. He is now Director of Clinical Research and Professor of Psychiatry at the University of South Florida College of Medicine in Tampa. He has pioneered in the study and treatment of the anxiety disease.